T0328446

Cambridge Elements ≡

Elements in Environmental Humanities
edited by
Louise Westling
University of Oregon
Serenella Iovino
University of North Carolina at Chapel Hill
Timo Maran
University of Tartu

THE VIRUS PARADIGM

A Planetary Ecology of the Mind

Roberto Marchesini
Center for the Study of Posthumanist Philosophy
(Translation by Sarah De Sanctis)

CAMBRIDGE
UNIVERSITY PRESS

CAMBRIDGE
UNIVERSITY PRESS

University Printing House, Cambridge CB2 8BS, United Kingdom

One Liberty Plaza, 20th Floor, New York, NY 10006, USA

477 Williamstown Road, Port Melbourne, VIC 3207, Australia

314–321, 3rd Floor, Plot 3, Splendor Forum, Jasola District Centre,
New Delhi – 110025, India

79 Anson Road, #06–04/06, Singapore 079906

Cambridge University Press is part of the University of Cambridge.

It furthers the University's mission by disseminating knowledge in the pursuit of
education, learning, and research at the highest international levels of excellence.

www.cambridge.org
Information on this title: www.cambridge.org/9781108965811
DOI: 10.1017/9781108966160

© Roberto Marchesini 2021

First published 2021

A catalogue record for this publication is available from the British Library.

ISBN 978-1-108-96581-1 Paperback
ISSN 2632-3125 (online)
ISSN 2632-3117 (print)

The Virus Paradigm

A Planetary Ecology of the Mind

Elements in Environmental Humanities

DOI: 10.1017/9781108966160
First published online: January 2021

Roberto Marchesini
Center for the Study of Posthumanist Philosophy
(Translation by Sarah De Sanctis)
Author for correspondence: Roberto Marchesini, Qbioetic@tin.it

Abstract: In recent years, the word "virus" has lost its biological perimeter of reference to acquire a much broader – one could say "paradigmatic" – meaning. The term "virus" can be seen as a key word or an explanatory model also for processes that go beyond the infectious sphere. Every event appears to have a viral character: from the way information is transmitted to the processes of cultural globalization, from the impact of human beings on the planet to the subversion of ecosystems, from pandemic risks to the demographic increase on the planet. This seems to be, indeed, the Age of the Virus. This model can be applied to most of the phenomena that characterize the twenty-first century. Its profile – its looming and invisible nature, its ability to use other people's resources to spread and to transform into a dangerous doppelganger – is perfect to represent the fears of the contemporary age.

Keywords: planetary risks, zoonoses, anthropocentrism, human nature, posthumanism

Isbns: 9781108965811 (PB), 9781108966160 (OC)
Issns: 2632-3125 (online), 2632-3117 (print)

Contents

1 A Virus for the Planet

1.1 Premise

The unbridled proliferation of human beings in recent centuries and their invasion of every last geographical corner resemble in many ways a pandemic, in terms both of its widespread character and its destructive effect. We use the term "Anthropocene" (Shantser 1973; Bonneuil & Frezzos 2013; Ellis 2018; Lewis & Maslin 2018), almost with barely concealed pride, to highlight the prevalence, if not the exclusivity, of our impact on Earth. We paint a picture of some sort of Human Era, which, unfortunately, on the one hand reveals our responsibility for the poor health of the planet, and on the other risks amplifying the anthropocentric idea that we are the undisputed rulers of Earth's dynamics, as we are emancipated from any ecological constraints. There is no doubt that our species has successfully achieved its adaptive affirmation: we have, in fact, colonized every corner of the globe, overcoming climatic and foraging adversities, defeating most of the dangers we met and reshaping the landscape according to our needs. However, it is precisely this expansion into the most varied places that makes our species more exposed to the current planetary imbalance. The transformation of each environment into a constrained habitat existing within certain limits does not shelter us from the alterations we cause. On the contrary, it exposes us to them even more. In other words, our success as a species – for example, from a demographic point of view – is the very reason why we should pay greater attention to ecological dynamics. The mistake we make, instead, is to believe that we are immune – closed off inside a bubble where technology acts as an amniotic container. This is why I have always been perplexed by the term "Anthropocene" because it lends itself to the most serious misunderstanding: that is, seeing ourselves as a world apart, freed from those ecological chains that sustain all species through interdependence. Our success, instead, has made us more dependent than ever!

We human beings seem to ignore the impact of our growth, behaving as if we were still a sparse population dispersed in the savannah of East Africa, carrying chipped stones and sticks, roaming in search of charred meat left over from a fire. And without the slightest worry, we are burning every last remaining corner of the world, infecting the lungs of the planet and filling the atmosphere with carbon dioxide. Are we a virus contaminating Gaia's exhausted body, to take up James Lovelock's metaphor (Lovelock 1979)? Can humankind be considered a silent deadly infection that now hails its virulence, its ill-fated success? There is undoubtedly a substantial difference between human action and that of a virus, which is due to the specific moral responsibility involved in our choices.

Bewilderment over our neglect of the network of living beings is growing day by day, paradoxically in direct proportion to the destructive power we are deploying. Even a virus owes its permanence to its ability to find a niche balance. The human species, on the contrary, risks applying the epidemic logic of the virus to the entire planet, without reaching or aspiring to a balance. But, in doing so, it is becoming Earth's disease.

The whole world is exhausted and feverish, upset by imbalanced meteorological phenomena and alterations in the trophic chains. In many ways, we are behaving like a virus, blindly replicating through the spasmodic use of the world's resources, disorganizing its structure and saturating it with debris. The planet thus seems to be seeking immunity to the human infection, because the entire biocenotic community is threatened by the ravenous aggression of humans. Our species consumes the world like an insatiable monster, capable of digesting the complex architecture of biodiversity, phagocytizing in a second the priceless masterpieces that emerged from the forge of time over millions of years thanks to a slow selective refinement. The impact of human development, tuned to the Promethean note of fire, leaves a trail of ash and deserts, destroying entire biological libraries so rich that the Library of Alexandria pales in comparison. Biodiversity contains galaxies of adaptive information, extraordinary life strategies accumulated in ecosystems thanks to the slow work of phylogeny. And we, with frightening arrogance, set fire to it, unaware that we are pulverizing knowledge on which our very future depends. The awareness of the morbidity of human action, present especially in younger generations, is therefore due to the erosion of a large part of the natural environment, which has occurred especially in recent decades (Spilsbury 2011; Renner 2013). Hence, the view of human species as a virus and the metaphorical use of the term "infection." We can try as hard as we please to deny our responsibility for the serious calamities that appear on our horizon like a looming storm, but today it is simply no longer possible to live in denial. Human responsibility for global warming – that is, the fever of the planet that, once again, brings us back to the virus metaphor – is recognized by the scientific community. Slowly, however, questions are also emerging in public opinion. It is wrong to generically blame the human species for what is happening, not recognizing the different impact of various populations, diverse cultural traditions and varying policies carried out by different states. And for the same reason, the word "anthropocene" is actually generic, because it tends to assign similar responsibilities to very different behaviors. Western culture has a major responsibility in this sense, due to its largely anthropocentric conception of the relationship with nature, which has transformed our impact on the planet into a sort of disease – hence the metaphor of viral infection. For this reason, I am very puzzled both by those who exalt human power to control the dynamics of nature, as if it were a machine with command levers, and by those who adhere to a sort of ahuman movement in favor of human extinction, forgetting the many virtues of our species. It is not a question of fighting humanity, but rather some aspects of the Western tradition, through a revolution of thought that is able to go beyond anthropocentrism.

After all, even if within a different axiological and interpretative framework, all those who consider their Selves as something disembodied – think about the idea of "mind-uploading" (Bostrom 2014) – can recognize themselves in the image of a virus. Those who aspire to a future of emancipation from the body, those who consider the human being as disconnected from the ecological networks of interdependence, those who see themselves as a world apart, as aboard a lifeboat that at any time can abandon the rest of the living to drift or shipwreck – those people are all viruses. Those who see the technosphere, which envelops the Anthropocene nucleus, as a sort of protein capsule that allows it to attack all nonhuman organisms, act just like a virus that hooks onto cell sites to inject its own replicating charge. People who think of the biosphere as a huge table where to feast *ad libitum* actually see themselves and behave as viruses, using technology as a capsid. Unfortunately, even this way of thinking, supported by an anthropocentric drift of humanist thought and formalized by the transhumanist movement, uses the virus paradigm as an explanatory model of the relationship between our species and the community of the living.

But how did we come to all this? It is difficult to identify a single cause or a linear chain of events that led us to this disastrous situation for the various biomes of our planet: either the problem lies in the natural demographic evolution of the human species, no longer kept under control by other competitors, or the critical factor is to be found in an anthropocentric culture that has devalued everything that did not belong to the human race. Perhaps both are to blame. What is certain is that today we are faced with a large number of critical issues: each one is highly significant in itself and all may converge to produce a catastrophic situation. What cannot, in any way, be questioned is the responsibility of human beings in this increasingly accelerated process of subversion (IPCC Report 2019; Houghton 2015). The victims of this process have been those self-regulating dynamics which, despite cyclical fluctuation and evolutionary events, still characterize life on Earth. This is an epochal event, unfortunately still denied or neglected by those who hold the reins of world governance in their hands, and this lack of awareness should be even more worrying. If life on Earth – which, as ecology has taught us, knows no barriers and represents the primary phenomenon of globalization – were an organism, we should now take a seat at its bedside and understand that we are the disease that is killing it.

The belief that our immediate interests should dictate our behavior has led us into a paradoxical condition, namely being the infection of our own planet. This infectious trend is now revealing all the serious problems it has created by altering the homeostatic systems that allowed for the development of life, including that of our own species, in the Cenozoic era. As a result of global warming, in addition to the systematic destruction of forests and the pollution of seas, we are also witnessing the loss of the biodiversity on which every living creature depends. If, on the other hand, we think that we are some sort of separate organism, we risk believing that we can save ourselves on our own and, in so doing, we risk pursuing this logic to its suicidal conclusion. The fact remains that we are part of an organism whose origin is rooted in the Tertiary rather than the Quaternary Period. The question is, are we really a virus for the Earth?

1.2 The Network of the Living

The best-known trait of viruses is undoubtedly their lack of interest in the host, even though the latter provides them with the opportunity for replication; in this sense, we can find several analogies between viruses and humans, if we look at the way the latter relate to the community of the living. A virus is an entity apparently free from belonging, it is neither rooted nor aspires to enter the network of ecological interdependencies, it is stateless and difficult to attribute. The etymology of the Latin word "virus" simply means poison, underlining the accidentality of its presence, that is, its nonintegration into the harmony of nature. In the history of life, the origin of viruses is not clear: according to some, they are the product of regressive processes of the genetic material, for others they may even be considered the first replicating forms in a hypothetical RNA world (Ben-Barak 2008; Fry 2000). Of course, like other living forms, viruses reproduce, have genetic material and evolve by natural selection, but in contrast they lack their own metabolism and cell structure. Viruses are undoubtedly borderline entities, capable of following the logic of living beings without, however, fully adhering to their laws. Humans, too, seem to want to free themselves from the laws of nature, to respond exclusively to their own expansionist dictates, transforming the world in to a frontier to conquer, in to a body to infect. The network of the living is inevitably made up of constraints, for the simple reason that every relationship produces chains of dependencies and limitations of usability, but the human imperative – we could say the Promethean legacy – is to circumvent all constraints, refusing to accept any external limitation.

The community of the living produces positions and denies existential volatility, because it roots each species in a niche, which gives it recognizability as well as a place to exist. But this is denied to human beings – as we read in Pico della Mirandola's *Oration on the Dignity of Man* (1942 [1496]) – or rather, it is rejected by humans themselves. The human being as it arises from the humanistic proposal eludes the great chain of living beings because it does not recognize itself in any rank, that is, in any adaptive niche, rejecting residence in the biotic community characteristic of all other species. Even generalist or opportunistic species present an adaptive conformation, which is denied to humans by the proponents of the theory of incompleteness. The nomadic habits of human beings lead them to massively exploit one territory, only to abandon it to move on to the next. Viruses use infected cells as a factory to reproduce indiscriminately and then spread from one host to another through the most diverse networks of contagion: blood, sputum, organic liquids. Viral dynamics resemble a fire that: i) feeds on fuel, that is, susceptible organisms; ii) gains strength through the convergence of triggers, that is, becomes virulent due to the recurrence of contagion; iii) spreads through the wind, which corresponds to the increase in contact in an epidemic. Social dynamics can be represented as infections, and our relationship with the biosphere replicates their stages. The network of the living, although denied by the human being, can be temporarily evaded, but in the end all the chickens come home to roost because one cannot hide from the laws that regulate the biosphere.

In order to understand the pressing issues we are facing, it is necessary to illustrate these self-regulatory dynamics that lead to a state of balance of powers and explain why they are being jeopardized today. As important physicists such as Erwin Schrödinger (1940) and Ilya Prigogine (1977) have shown, life is a thermodynamic process of accumulation and dissipation of the Sun's radiant energy. Throughout the history of life on our planet, this process has produced complex organisms that, over the course of generations, have given rise to phenomena of evolution correlative to their life environments. It's what we now call "adaptation" – a process of specialization of the various life-forms, whereby each species is linked to a certain environment and a certain way of life. The study of ecology shows how the biocenotic community forms a network of relationships where each species is connected to the others through several interdependencies. It is a mistake to consider a species in an essentialistic way, that is, as a package of self-referenced qualities, because each character is expressed through this relationship network. Therefore, we must never forget that the biosphere is also a global network that is self-organized on several levels, from the elementary one of the cell to the ultimate one of the macro-organism called Gaia.

The organization of the living at different levels is based on homeostatic mechanisms of negative feedback interaction, so that the growth of a factor induces the development of a counter-factor capable of containing its impact. We know, for example, that: i) the population increase of herbivores is held back by carnivores and, vice versa, the numbers of the latter are constrained by that of herbivores; ii) the production of carbon dioxide by animals is controlled by plants' intake of this gas through photosynthesis; iii) the organic material of the carcasses of living creatures is brought back into circulation by detritivores. This food web (Smith & Smith 2006; Odum & Barret 2005) or life cycle reminds us that, despite being subject to fluctuations, the system tends to stay within certain gradients. Even the evolution of the living can be read as a convergence on homeostatic and relational organizations, whereby each organism depends for survival on an ad hoc environment and its anatomical and functional conformation requires certain parameters. In the same way, each species is related to the others through chains of complex interactions. Every time a link in the network is cut off, the whole chain of interdependencies is put at risk, because no organism is isolated.

The system obviously has some resilience – this is true for cells as well as for other higher-level networks – so that small and gradual perturbations that do not involve points of particular sensitivity are buffered. What is worrying, regarding human action, is precisely this quality. Let me clarify: Homeodynamic systems, capable of keeping variables within a given gradient range, precisely *because* they absorb perturbations inevitably end up hiding their effects and therefore do not immediately reflect the actual degree of the damage. Many of these are "threshold systems" (Marchesini 1996a), that is, capable of operating by negative feedback below a certain value (like a thermostat) and then behaving in an autocatalytic way, that is, by positive feedback above that value. Let's take an example: Up to a certain concentration limit, the carbon dioxide produced by heterotrophic organisms stimulates the growth of plants and marine organisms able to lower the amount of the said gas, which means that we have a balanced or negative feedback system; however, above that limit, the excess of carbon dioxide favors global warming by the greenhouse effect, decreasing the development of plants and also increasing the frequency of fires and the destruction of plankton, with further release of carbon dioxide. Suddenly, a condition that was partly compensated for through buffering effects leads to events that accentuate it – with a catastrophic outcome – as a result of positive feedback. Not to mention other phenomena of greenhouse gas release due to glacier melt.

Homeodynamic systems develop over biological times, that is, over tens of millions of years, and are incomprehensible if evaluated by the yardstick of historical time, which is our focal point and which struggles to cope even with periods of thousands of years. These systems are very effective and efficient in building a sort of stable macroclimate – such as that of a rainforest – but precisely because of the complex chains of relationships that regulate their functions, they are extremely vulnerable to major disturbances, as shown by the frequent mass extinctions that have characterized life on Earth (Gould 1991; Buffetaut 1993). Human beings are irresponsibly pushing the homeostatic thresholds of the planet and are doing so by acting on different fronts and in different ways that, unfortunately, converge on the same perturbative direction. First of all, there is a progressive subversion of some cycles that are fundamental for the balance of life – such as water, nitrogen, carbon – due to activities directly or indirectly related to human action. Agronomic pressure, for example, due to the energy-intensive diet of Western and developing countries – I am referring to the massive use of food of animal origin – has produced progressive deforestation that has affected the last remaining rainforests on Earth, transforming them into pastures or monocultures for fodder. As we know, forests represent the most important bastion of carbon dioxide uptake and oxygen release. Unfortunately, the past decade has been disastrous in this respect: in 2019 alone, over 20 million hectares are estimated to have gone up in smoke (Mariotti 2019). The effects of this are having repercussions on many nodes of the network of the living.

As stated, forests are crucial for the carbon cycle and therefore for limiting the greenhouse effect. Destroying them not only means canceling out their function as the lungs of the planet and as tools for the removal of greenhouse gases, but also means increasing the concentration of carbon dioxide itself, thereby exacerbating global warming. At the same time, the destruction of places where biodiversity is at its highest – most of the species present in such ecosystems are not even included in the known catalog of the living – is leading to the so-called "sixth mass extinction" (Kolbert 2014). This is not a minor problem and it concerns not only disappearing species, but also those that remain, because they are being disconnected from those biocenotic relationships that safeguard their balance. These self-regulating mechanisms are often mistaken for static systems, but obviously this is not the case. A biocenosis is a dynamic system of regulations within fluctuations that are sometimes cyclical, sometimes evolutionary, but that always involve interactive convergence between organisms. I am therefore concerned not only about the species that are going to die out today, but also about those that will disappear over time and, even more so, about the species that will see a population boom that will no longer be contained, condemning the entire biome to decline and initiating dangerous animal diseases that will inevitably pose a widespread danger.

1.3 Deforestation

One of the phenomena of greatest impact on the balance of the planet, and therefore on the maintenance of the network of interdependencies that characterize the life of Gaia as it was configured in the Tertiary era, can be traced back to the massive use of the territory for anthropic purposes. Since the Neolithic revolution, which began about 10,000 years ago, at first slowly and then feverishly, humans have carried out the most devastating operation that Earth has ever seen: the replacement of forests with land intended for the exclusive use of human beings. The processes that have contributed most to deforestation have been livestock farming and agriculture, in addition, of course, to housing and urban conversion, that is, the so-called overbuilding. However, the role of agro-zootechnics has been predominant: when chainsaws are put into operation or a forest burns down, there is always a plan to create new pastures or land for cultivation (Rifkin 1993; Sachs 2011). In the human imagination, deforestation means translating an unproductive resource into a fruitful mine, in the immediate term through timber (which is useful in many productive activities) and in the future thanks to the fertility of the soil and its high value in terms of humus, to obtain both lush pastures and land for agronomic activity. The felling of trees then accelerated dramatically in the 20th century, when tractors and other mechanical means were involved in tillage and harvesting. It was at that point that even the tree-studded hedges that delimited different plots were cut down, transforming the countryside into stretches of open land that go as far as the eye can see (Mazzino & Ghersi 2003).

This process was slow and gradual up to the threshold of the modern age – many historians consider the 11th century as the transition phase in the transformation of the European landscape (Andreoli & Montanari 1995) – and then continued at an exponential pace. Today the incidence of this phenomenon has unfortunately reached a worrying peak, as over the past century the last remaining rainforests have been ravaged for extensive farming and monocultures. In order to cultivate an area, in fact, one has to carry out certain operations – such as weeding, changing the course of rivers, plowing the soil – that have a considerable impact on biodiversity and fertility itself. The forest environment is the result of an ecological climax that has taken an unimaginable amount of time to form and yet it is swept away in a flash, first by chainsaws, then by plows. The forest has its own homeostasis, where trees are at the center of a network of self-organizing processes: roots expand into the ground to avoid erosion, leaves fall and feed a complex system of water retention, nitrogen-fixing bacterial colonies increase fertility, plants transpire to feed the formation of vapor and an organic layer gives rise to humus. Deforestation inevitably produces aridity and deletion of the organic part of the soil: the geographical areas where trees were first cut down are now deserts (Lanternari 2003; Imeson 2012).

We may believe that in these geographical areas, once the cradle of great civilizations – think, for example, of the Fertile Crescent – meteorological dynamics have simply changed in the direction of aridity, and perhaps this is indeed the case. In fact, we know that over time air currents change also on the basis of the modification of tectonic plates. However, today it is well known that, in the rainforests, it is the plants themselves that create that recycling of water that prevents desertification. The Amazonian forest contributes to feeding the humid and rainy climate that distinguishes it, so it is increasingly evident that it is nature itself that packages its environmental qualities over time (Campbell, Reece & Simon 2007). When a rainforest is cut down, water is dispersed by runoff, the humus layer is pulverized, the habitats built by a large number of organisms (niche construction) are destroyed, the most important climatic cycles (water, nitrogen, carbon) are permanently broken down and the soil maintained by the root system is eroded. How can we fail to see the forest as a mortally infected macroorganism?

The erosive processes occurring in natural habitats are strikingly reminiscent of the evolution of epidemics. At first, they only affect some areas – generally the most promising ones that are healthy but also fertile and rich in water – and then they spread in one main direction and along secondary offshoots until they affect the whole territory. Deforestation is always accompanied by misleading publicity, so that the forest is painted as obscure, elusive and threatening, a receptacle of feral and demonic entities, while the felling of the trees is dotted with brightness and clarity, irenic in its submission to human control. The conversion of the "saltus" into cultivated land is seen as an operation of reclamation or purification, because it overlaps simplification with essentiality, by stamping out wilderness in line with the best prophylaxis. When it is not chainsaws, it is fire that devastates the forests, always set by human beings, most of the time for petty interests, sometimes by neglect, occasionally for fun. The Promethean myth that portrays our species as indebted to Prometheus – the reflective Titan who bestowed fire on the human being – binds us indissolubly not only to *techne* but also to fire. This story, in my opinion, has a strong anthropological and psychological significance. When Edward O. Wilson (2017) locates the origin of myths in the nocturnal tales exchanged by hunters beside the fire, he captures an aspect that should make us think: the fascination we get from flames is perhaps an ancestral trait, a sort of resonance that, if on the one hand captures our attention in front of pyrotechnics and screens, on the other hand exposes us to pyromania (113–119).

Of course, what should also be of concern is the disarticulation of ecosystems with very serious repercussions on animal populations, both in terms of demographic balance and habitat displacement. Human beings have already contributed – directly, through the marketing of exotic species, and indirectly, through the exchange of goods – to importing numerous alien species that have put ecological sustainability at serious risk. But there is also an epidemiological threat: the transfer of viral pathogens from one species to another, including humans. The ecological alteration, creating a magmatic situation of cohabitations unknown in phylogeny, leads to the development of highly infectious zoonoses that are difficult to eradicate. We must not forget that a biome is not simply a set of environmental components hosting a series of living organisms: we must rather imagine it as a network of interdependencies that maintains particular values within a certain gradient. When we break this network, the whole system breaks down and changes the mobility of the factors at stake, especially the infectious ones, which were previously confined and contained at one point of the network.

Deforestation also shows us the human being's inability to cope with long timescales. Destroying a forest does not mean destroying something that refers to the here and now, but rather an entity that has been created over time, in some cases over tens of thousands years, and which would take just as long to be reformed – provided that it is ever possible to reform it, I would add.

1.4 Consumerist Bulimia

One of the most important causes of the anthropic conversion of forest and wooded areas is certainly the need to find more and more food resources for the human population. We might, then, believe that what we are observing is nothing other than the consequence of the uncontrolled development of humanity, and in some ways this is true. As we know, the demographic development of our species has followed an impressive growth rate over the last two centuries: if in the nineteenth century the world population was still around one billion, by the 1960s it had already reached three billion, doubling in just forty years, reaching six billion at the end of the 1990s. But it only took a decade to grow by more than a billion and, even if it has an irregular trend, this development rate seems not to have come to a halt. It is inevitable that this phenomenon will have an impact on the consumption of resources, such as the increase in fishing, which is putting the regenerative capacities of the oceans to the test. The unstoppable growth of the world's population, especially in some geographical areas, is causing the depletion of resources and the use of all types of animals for food. The markets of megacities, where no attention is paid to hygiene, are becoming open-air epidemic factories.

Everywhere forests are being cut down in order to obtain areas to be used for agro-zootechnical purposes, so that not only are we increasingly coming into contact with animal populations that were previously confined in their environment, but we are also forcing them to colonize human spaces to find food. Indeed, the human being not only massively exploits the resources, but also produces a large amount of waste, such as to convert more and more wild species to synanthropy. Seagulls, for instance, have abandoned coastal areas to move to the city: they are only the most striking example of a phenomenon that involves not only birds but also many mammals, such as foxes, wolves, raccoons, bears, bats and beech martens (Cignini 2019; Mainardi 2016; Marchesini 1998). It is incredible to observe the invasiveness of our species, its ability to occupy any space and feed on any living thing, but what is even more impressive is the tendency to convert the metabolism of the entire biosphere in an anthropic sense, just like a virus that enters a cell and reprograms it for its own replication. The most striking example of this conversion flow is the transformation of agricultural.

There is no doubt that population growth has played a role in this increased conversion, and we must ask ourselves whether we should not give serious thought to the risks of the demographic bomb, which, among other things, is a possible cause of highly virulent epidemics (Ehrlich 1995). Yet what is being flaunted by the governments of many states is still the importance and the need to increase the birth rate, in a logic that cannot fail to recall that of a virus. Patriarchal cultures, which dominate the post-Neolithic milieu, oppose all forms of female emancipation, trying to impose on women the sole role of motherhood, de facto transforming them into a reproductive resource. Demographic warfare becomes ideology, imposing the selfishness of the genetic affirmation on reason: we are thus witnessing growth that seems out of control.

Yet, the agronomic pressure should not be attributed solely to the population boom, however significant, but also to the *type* of food consumed by Western and developing countries, particularly China (Environmental Working Group 2011; Food and Agriculture Organization of the United States 2019; The Guardian 2009). In nature, carnivores are at the top of the food pyramid, and therefore there are fewer of them: the reason for this is essentially related to energy. In order to transform vegetable proteins into animal proteins, the conversion index is around the generic value of 10:1, which means that excessive use of these foods is highly energy-intensive, thus requiring a wide availability of agricultural land on which to plant forage monocultures. We know that in Europe and North America, in the space of a century, we have gone from consuming 20 kilograms (44 pounds) of meat per head per year to 80/100 kilograms (175/220 pounds) per head per year, and it is no mystery that the majority of farmland is being used to produce not food for humans, but fodder. This leads to ever-increasing agronomic pressure, causing the destruction of forests, but also: i) massive use of pesticides, increasingly impacting on the entomofauna (e.g., the progressive decrease in pollinators and entomophagous insects); iii) subsidence of the land, which is crushed by agricultural machinery, after being depleted of humus by increasingly deep plowing processes; iii) soil erosion, especially in hilly and rainy areas, because the eradication of the root network produces landslides and impoverishes the organic substratum, with subsequent desertification. It sounds like a war bulletin, and it should, because we are not only attacking the territory to make it agricultural, but we are also reducing the fertility of the soil.

The massive rearing of cattle, pigs and poultry, in addition to sustaining this appalling agronomic pressure, is one of the main sources of environmental pollution and of depletion of resources, including water. After all, the ongoing ecological problems can be summarized in terms of pollution rate, resource depletion, alteration of biocenotic networks and decrease in biodiversity. There is no doubt that livestock surplus is responsible for all these disturbing factors, in addition to being a dangerous factory of viral zoonoses and antibiotic-resistant bacterial strains (Tibon-Cornillot & Andremont 2007; Drlica & Perlin 2011; Kon & Ray 2016). Above all, the phenomenon of hospital-acquired infections is particularly alarming. I am not playing prophet of doom – it is simply undeniable that keeping a large number of animals in conditions of suffering and constraint in small spaces facilitates the onset of viroses that can be transferred to our species, as already happened with rinder-pest which gave rise to measles. In addition, the extensive use of prophylactic and auxinic antibiotics – used to increase production (Piva et al. 1999) – determines the phenomenon of antibiotic resistance, taking away the last weapon we have to combat bacterial infections. The dietary style we have adopted contributes to this impressive agronomic pressure, which is endanger-ing the homeostasis of the planet, biodiversity, the fertility of the soil and also the ecological chains on which our very survival depends.

A reconsideration of our lifestyle is therefore of vital importance, because it is not possible to fight for the defense of the environment while ignoring the underlying causes of the situation. We need an ecology for the mind that is able to highlight the contradictions underlying our way of thinking about our daily existence and everyday *Dasein*. Setting the self-fulfillment of the individual as an existential end, claiming for oneself all the meanings of life, has created loneliness and suffering, in addition to taking the worst instincts of hedonism and survival to their highest level. The liquidity of society (Bauman 2000) and relationships, in the name of a sort of ego-theism, is not only the cause of everything that – multiplied by billions of people – has produced the environmental disaster we are facing, but also our condemnation, because we will never find meaning in a life that, isolated from all relationships, inevitably proves to be a disposable void.

2 Pandemics and Individual Freedoms

2.1 Premise

The Covid-19 epidemic (SARS-CoV-2) has confronted us with a planetary emergency that we were unprepared for, as can be clearly seen in every area: psychology, society, economics and – above all – biopolitics (Butler 2020a, 2020b, 2016). The onset of the pandemic has certainly led to the emergence of unexpected community cohesions, unusual expressions of solidarity and surprising supplementary responses, but at the same time it has provoked behaviors imbued with prejudice and frankly unacceptable from an ethical point of view. Also, the most fanciful conjectures have been made about absurd conspiracy theories, such as the concealment of the effects of 5 G technology, the bacteriological war between the United States and China, the manufacture of an engineered virus that escaped from a laboratory in Wuhan, the implementation of the epidemic by a pharmaceutical company to get rich through the sale of the vaccine, the pandemic as a pretext to establish a world dictatorship, the governmental excuse of prophylactic control to eliminate individual freedoms, world speculation by the financial elites and even the arrival of aliens. Such fantasies deserve to be enunciated only as a litmus test of the human need to attribute every calamity to a precise external reason, shunning both the idea of randomness (chance, to which we are all inevitably exposed) and human responsibility for the increase in risk factors. This aspect, as we shall see, is far from irrelevant.

It is clear, then, that the pandemic should not only be tackled through the lens of epidemiology, despite the obvious importance of the latter. Rather, one should also take into account the social dynamics that it triggers, the changes it produces in the collective imagination and the very way in which it is narrated. The pandemic has set in motion figurative processes that cannot be ignored for their high heuristic value. Ian Alan Paul, professor at the College of Arts and Sciences at SUNY Stony Brook, in his article "The Corona Reboot" (2020a) claimed that, on the one hand, the pandemic has caused strong deceleration or even extinction of traditional productive activities and social conviviality dynamics based on somatic presence and, on the other hand, it has accelerated or even justified more intense forms of digital connection, that is, it has catalyzed the advent of a new type of society based on digital subjectivity.

Like a computer being reprogrammed, human society is experiencing, albeit forcibly, a system reboot involving the human condition on a planetary scale. The pandemic would therefore be a caesura, a threshold between a "before" and an "after", capable of establishing a new world where control, deterritorialization, the domestication of the subject imposed by interconnection and the digital economy open up different scenarios from those we are used to. In other words, there is a growing feeling that after the pandemic, nothing will be the same as before.

2.2 Narrating the Pandemic

Life in the time of coronavirus has a thousand facets, made up of recurring images and words such as "viral", interviews with a wide variety of opinion leaders and heated debates. The first thing that changed is the terminology in use, which instils an attitude of attention, suspicion, distance, war, martyrdom, cohesion: a free-flow of thoughts and words that has transformed people's daily lives to the point of even affecting their dreams (Žižek 2020). The virus thus becomes a paradigm of everyday living. The most obvious metamorphosis of the social symposium is precisely this digital ellipse, a trend that had already spread in the previous twenty years, mainly thanks to the advent of social media and smartphones, but which now, due to the risk of infection, becomes an unavoidable necessity, changing people's habits and inaugurating new economies. The narrative, therefore, seems to satisfy the desire for stupefaction and future projection, in the eagerness to identify caesuras in the course of history and to foretell the dawning of new age, rather than accepting the fact that we are living within an unpredictable flow of events that follow chaotic dynamics (Làzlò 2006). Once again we need to engage in mythopoesis and imagine ourselves as part of an epic story, marked by the voyeuristic pleasure of being able to witness a somehow grandiose spectacle.

People photograph the empty, magnificent and ghostly cities, immortalizing them from all perspectives, with the help of drones or from their balconies, which have become the proscenium of new forms of social relationships. This inaugurates a real aesthetics of the infection, which transforms the old town centers, emptied of people and cars, into postcards dominated by the illuminated monuments, the streets reflecting the solitary glow of the moon and the stealthy passage of wild animals. The pandemic sublime has thus become a style that arouses wonder and fear, dopamine and adrenaline, and draws a portrait of metropolitan spaces completely subverted in their meaning. The cities, still recognizable, bear the vivid image of something that remains unchanged, in its stone geometries, as opposed to human transitoriness, in a sort of reversal of postwar horizons where people swarmed around buildings in ruins (Pievani 2019). We have the sensation of being deprived of our own world, like mollusks extracted by force from their shells.

TV news programs are filled with images that act as icons of this tragic moment, such as Pope Francis praying in a deserted St. Peter's Square, thousands of people fleeing New Delhi, sanitization activities along the streets of Seoul or long lines of military trucks carrying bodies for cremation. In this way we learn about the practices of forced ventilation, intubation and pronation, as well as the terrible lifeboat logic (Hardin 1974) at stake whenever a doctor has to choose who to care for based on the crude calculation of life expectancy. It is then that the virosis becomes paradigmatic, because it throws in our faces a mountain of questions that require new descriptive and explanatory forms, real quantum leaps of explanations to be given to others and to ourselves.

The theme of nature taking up the spaces abandoned by the human being, in line with the descriptions of the ecological transformations that took place in Chernobyl, returns in many videos shared on social media showing deer, badgers, wolves and bears walking peacefully through the city streets. In her 1962 book *Silent Spring*, Rachel Carson showed us how the massive use of pesticides had silenced the American countryside due to the destruction of the avifauna. In the same way, today humans are experiencing a new silent spring, which, however, concerns their own estrangement from the areas that they inhabit. The narration of the environment deprived of the constant and frenetic presence of the human being reminds us of Alan Weisman's book *The World Without Us* (2007), where the author describes an interesting thought experiment on how the rest of nature would react if suddenly human beings disappeared because of a natural or produced virus. Cities now seem to confirm his view.

We suddenly have the impression of a déja-vu, of a story already heard. It brings to mind an experiment published in *Nature Medicine* in November 2015, entitled "A Sars-like Cluster of Circulating Bat Coronaviruses Shows Potential for Human Emergence," carried out and coordinated by Professor Ralph S. Baric of the University of North Carolina at Chapel Hill, in which a coronavirus originating from the *Rhinolophus sinicus* bat had been modified in its infectious binding proteins. The idea that the infection was produced by humans, and in particular by scientists with the complicity of governments – the former for the Faustian desire to play God, the latter for even more prosaic applications – exerts a degree of fascination. As in all narratives, it is necessary to identify a culprit and a plot, in order to turn the whole thing into a thriller.

After all, there is nothing new about the topos of an apocalyptic pandemic, caused by terrorist attacks or chimerical viruses escaped from laboratories, with humanity forced to retreat into artificial environments, most often underground. This idea won over the general public with two films, both from 1995: *12 Monkeys* directed by Terry Gilliam and *Outbreak* directed by Wolfgang Petersen. But it was in the first decade of the twenty-first century that the theme of the pandemic established itself as a real cinematic genre, where the contagion merged with broader dystopian scenarios. This kind of narrative is often about the development of a terrible pandemic that rapidly spreads all over the globe starting from circumscribed episodes, so as to transform the anonymous viral expansion into a succession of events. It is then interesting to take up what Ian Alan Paul said in *Ten Premises for a Pandemic* (2020b), namely that "A pandemic isn't a collection of viruses, but is a social relation among people, mediated by viruses." In fact, in many of these films the infected human being does not disappear or die, but is transformed into something else, mixing the narrative register with another genre, that of zombie stories.

The image of the zombie is a stereotype that is being asserted to describe the infected community, to recount the daily bulletin of the infected and the dead. And as in a film by John Carpenter or George Romero, the asymptomatic nature of the infected person creates a climate of suspicion but also of unrecognizability of the neighbor, who is now experienced as probably dangerous or as a plague spreader. The narrative of social distancing represents a further aspect with a strong impact that shows how, beyond the various ramblings on the new virtual identity of the individual, we remain indissolubly social animals that need a somatic participation in the symposium. The relationship between a patient and a doctor who is completely covered up becomes even more inhumane, to the point of inaugurating the use of robots: through a screen, patients can dialogue with healthcare staff free of masks or other vestments that reduce access to facial mimicry. The latter, regardless of all our claims to emancipation from nature, represents our deep roots in the primate community. People hidden behind a mask lose their human recognizability: they become zombies from which to stay away and with which there can be no empathic communication made of smiles and winks.

2.3 The Fall of Freedoms

Especially in some countries, the health emergency has called for repressive measures and promoted, at times, the legitimization of authoritarian drifts (Agamben 2020; O'Farrell 2020). We have thus witnessed, albeit in different ways in each State, a weakening of democratic practices and a centralization of the executive. Either governments claimed full power, or at least they implemented a regime of close supervision of the people and a reduction in parliamentary prerogatives, accompanied by tighter control of the media. Democracies have shown a particular degree of vulnerability in the face of the outbreak of the epidemic: this was expressed in the unfortunately still widespread prejudice that they are largely unable to deal with urgent decisions that need to be taken in a timely and firm manner. This is a mistake, of course, because a pandemic requires, on the one hand, an increase in individual information and awareness and, on the other, collective participation, because everyone's behavior is key to the effectiveness of any response.

As a side effect, this led to the use of military terminology, as if we were really fighting a war. Hence the many references to battle strategies: doctors in the trenches, the contagion front, our casualties, the battle against the infectious army, the curfew or lockdown (Cassandro 2020; Solidoro 2020; Sontag 1978). The military narrative also presents the paradox of shifting responsibility for the situation onto an external enemy, which is not only hostile but also alien to us. The war rhetoric not only exalts a cohesive and heroic "us", but also stigmatizes a treacherous enemy who has deliberately attacked us in order to annihilate us. But this is not so, of course: the representation of the infection as an army that has invaded us is misleading for various reasons – the most important being that it leads us to disregard our own responsibility for the infection (Quammen 2012: 43–49). The pandemic, in fact, is nothing more than a fairly predictable result of a series of alterations that have been produced in the network of life. The idea that the entire biosphere is nothing more than a set of passive resources at our unlimited disposal, and with which we are not implicated in the slightest, makes it impossible for us to understand the pandemic: that is why we treat it as a sort of external, alien and accidental invasion, which cannot be traced back to the global model we call capitalism.

As suggested by Frank M. Snowden, historian of epidemics at Yale University and author of *Epidemics and Society* (2019), epidemics reflect the fragilities and contradictions of certain social models, acting as "detectors" of the vulnerabilities within them. If cholera showed the limits of nineteenth-century urbanism and the poor health and hygiene rules in the poor suburbs inhabited by the massified working class, the Spanish influenza of the early postwar period of the twentieth century mirrored the wartime disasters that had struck the world, with its concentration camps and the ensuing famine. In an interview by Stella Levantesi (2020) that appeared in the Italian newspaper Il Manifesto, Snowden pointed out that the Covid-19 pandemic reflects four main factors: the destruction of the environment, the demographic boom, the speed of movement and inequalities. These, in fact, are the issues that should be on the political agenda and that make up the correct interpretation of what is happening. On the contrary, we are looking for scapegoats, we invoke a single leader and an authoritarian regime, while wondering when we will finally be able to resume our usual habits. The pandemic, instead, should make us reflect on the failure of the development model undertaken especially in the last century and on the tangible impossibility of continuing along that path.

The virus should indeed dictate a paradigmatic revision of our life model, showing us the causes that have brought us into this situation, revealing the fragilities that the pandemic has simply brought to light and finally offering us the possibility of changing the model, even as far as the relationship between body and society. A pandemic travels through our bodies, so any intervention of epidemiological prophylaxis inevitably becomes a form of biopolitics, to follow Michel Foucault (1961). In fact, we have witnessed new forms of alienation, inaugurating specific practices of body management, regulation of people's biological lives and monopolistic control of those aspects of physicality to which we never thought we would be subjected. Cloistering, however, goes beyond confinement and social distancing and becomes an interference in the very expression of bodily life. The virus has highlighted our animality (Le Moli 2020), bringing to the surface repressed fragments that inevitably clash with the idea of emancipation from nature that had led us to believe that the body, reified into controlled flesh, was only that of other animals. What is waning is a whole ontological paradigm and not just a social and economic model: perhaps this is why it is frightening, because it has profound, I would say foundational implications.

The lockdown transformed the entire globe into a sort of maximum-security prison, where every exit, if not documented by imperative requirements, turned the individual into a delinquent. The logic of control and denouncing has therefore found fertile ground, fueling feelings of suspicion and intolerance, resentment and bitterness, which are often derived from racism. This is a very serious phenomenon which has already been recorded during previous epidemics, but in the case of Sars-CoV2 it was accentuated by the fact that it developed in a very specific geographical area and can be attributed to food practices which are equally identifiable from a cultural point of view. In short, therefore, scapegoats were sought and everyone became a sort of judge and jury of others' behavior, as in the dystopian world of Ray Bradbury's *Fahrenheit 451* (2013).

The epidemiological crisis seems, on the one hand, to lower the collective capacity to express dissent and, on the other, to build a sort of passive acceptance of authoritarian drifts that are expressed through the strengthening of police forces and the elimination of all critical voices (Applebaum 2020; Luca 2020). There is no doubt that the risk of contagion is real, but it is clear that this fact entails transformations in social dynamics that deserve careful reflection. We hear of the South Korean model as the first form of strict digital control of citizens, through applications able to follow the movements and therefore the very life of people, including their relationships, in total disregard of any right to privacy. Control over people has become a sensational topic in the course of the pandemic, but it has only made explicit – or better, visible – a process that was already underway with the self-imposed traceability of the individual in terms of transactions made, things bought online, places visited and routes taken, interests shown in consulting certain websites, affiliation groups chosen on social media, participation in eBay auctions, accessibility to bank accounts, use of digital currency, etc. (Solove 2004: 93–127). The great life companion of the twenty-first-century person, the smartphone, is in fact the most formidable of bugs, making our lives trackable at all times and forcing us into a sort of permanent connection. And it is precisely the smartphone that triggers the project of epidemiological control of the person.

On a different note, the pandemic risks deeply undermining the global economy, not by acting like the 2008 financial crisis, but by affecting the real economy, creating geopolitical upheavals of epochal proportions. It can already be seen that certain supranational institutions, such as the European Union, are increasingly struggling to hold together the centrifugal thrusts of its various member countries, and this will lead to transformations that are difficult to predict but will certainly be significant. As I have said, the kind of economy that has characterized the past century has run up against environmental resource constraints, a problem that was already in evidence before the advent of coronavirus (Caffo 2020). The issue of global warming, neglected by the agenda of the rulers of the most important States responsible for the carbon dioxide emissions, had already shown its effects on a planetary level. The Covid-19 virus has done nothing more than shutting down the engines of the human machine, allowing us – perhaps – to reflect on a different type of economy that needs to be implemented as soon as possible.

It is evident that the economy cannot be detached from people's lives, from their way of assigning value to something and not to something else, from the list of prerogatives that the individual arrogates to themselves, from the style that they adopt even in the form of ordinary resource consumption. For this reason, no economy is ever an end in itself, but is always at the service of a collective life project based on certain values. Likewise, we can no longer conceive of an economy that does not take due account of the environmental impact of its practices, ignoring the fact that it responds to network logics that transcend state borders and have repercussions that do not stop at our arbitrary customs offices. Individual spaces and natural resources are therefore two converging terms in the economic fabric: any reflection on what model to adopt cannot but adhere to it.

If we understand freedom as feeling free from environmental compatibility, as a green light to unbridled hedonism, not worrying about future generations and believing that the only thing worth existing for is to consume as much as possible ... then I believe we should wake up as soon as possible, because the reality check will not be imposed by the virus but by the world itself. The freedom of the Western individual, coming out of the second half of the twentieth century, has been understood as a progressive emancipation from any form of restriction which, if on the one hand has sanctioned greater self-awareness and ownership rights, on the other has made us compulsive consumers incapable of accepting any limit. We are accustomed to believing that the environmental crisis is someone else's doing, only blaming governments or economic powers for the situation. Without denying their responsibility, and being aware of the different levels of impact of the instituted directives, it is also clear that the robbery economy that characterizes Western and emerging countries is also the result of choices that people make in the name of individual well-being. Fossil fuel consumption, food based on animal products, the production of non-biodegradable waste and wild overbuilding are the foundations of an economy that is no longer sustainable, and the virus is certainly not what is threatening it (Mason 2005). We need a different way of considering our lives, starting from the basic approach to mobility and food and leaving behind the role of mindless consumers, because there is no more room for those who think only of eroding resources in total dissociation from recycling, saving and sustainable choices.

2.4 Zoonoses

Diseases transmissible from other species to humans account for about 60% of all pathogens affecting us, and it is estimated that the new zoonotic waves that have affected humans have caused tens of millions of deaths over the last forty years. Zoonoses are a key chapter in epidemiology, and veterinary sciences have played a central role in their control, especially in relation to domestic animals (Bauerfeind et al. 2016). Unfortunately, since the second half of the twentieth century, we have witnessed a crescendo of zoonoses and epidemic outbreaks throughout the world, creating extremely dangerous situations. The new zoonoses, in fact, are for the most part – we estimate over 70% – linked to pathogens derived from wild animals, which shows that we are faced with a problem that is not only epidemiological, but also ecological. The destruction of the environment, caused by deforestation and climate change, has favored contacts with wild species – many of which are natural reservoirs of some viruses with which they have established adaptive balances – favoring spillover, that is, the passing of the infection into the human host, inaugurating real epidemic hotspots. The succession of these episodes indicates a sort of viral ecology – a virosphere – which, upset by the changes caused by our species on the network of living creatures, is giving rise to catastrophic processes. The impressive predictions contained in David Quammen's (2012: 45) book *Spillover* go in this direction. In it, he wonders what the Next Big Zoonosis will be: "Will the Next Big One come out of a rainforest or a market in southern China?"

The consumption of wild animals has played a key role in recent epidemics – for example, in Africa for the Ebola filovirus or in Eastern wet markets for the Sars coronavirus (Sars-CoV). Indeed, as Quammen himself suggests, without doubt such events cannot be dismissed as mere accidents, because they mirror the convergence of an ecological and epidemiological crisis. In other words, the cross-species transmission of pathogens must be understood by focusing more on human responsibility: on the one hand, by destroying a large part of the world's ecosystems we created magmatism in the virosphere; on the other hand, demographic evolution, the development of large pockets of poverty in some populations, the concentration of people in vast metropolises, the processes of globalization and the widespread technologies of human mobility all contribute to the spread of contagions.

Sometimes an epidemic develops through triangulation with domestic animals, as in the case of the paramyxovirus Hendra, which in the 1990s generated a zoonosis in Australia, passing from flying foxes – frugivorous bats of the *Pteropus* genus – to horses, and from them to humans. In this epidemic, it was noticed that people who were in contact with the bats did not get infected, but grooms and vets did: this was because horses amplified the microbial load, due to their species-specific susceptibility to the virus. This suggests two considerations: i) beyond the risk of contagion, we must acknowledge different infectious exposure in different species, so that a pet can play the role of epidemiological sounding board; ii) the greater the ecological cohabitation with the reservoir species, in this case greater in humans than in horses – introduced just over two centuries ago in Australia – the lower the infectious risks, so that a higher viral concentration is necessary to produce the disease. On the other hand, from this we cannot draw the conclusion that domestic animals always play a role in intensifying the viral load because, on the contrary, sometimes the presence in them of similar strains to the human virus enables cross-immunity (Diamond 1997). We therefore need to adopt an ecological perspective.

It follows, then, that the environmental issue is central to the epidemiological assessment. Like a fire, the infection rips through the new host and then seems to disappear, but in the case of zoonoses – unlike exclusively human pathologies such as smallpox – there can be no eradication, because the infectious agent resides in the reservoir species and in complex networks of interaction between species that share a given ecosystem. Therefore, the trans-specific passage – when a virus learns to attack subjects of another species – is more problematic, because in these situations the epidemic seems to hatch from the ashes and appear at different times and in different areas, as in the case of the Ebola virus. And it is in such moments that humans are confronted with the narrowness of their time window compared to the long biological times of phylogenetic adaptation. After all, the infectious mechanism responds to the same principles of evolution and adaptation to which living beings are subjected and, like other processes of interaction, such as predation or symbiosis, builds networks of ecological balances with the living organisms with which the viruses live. Zoonoses do not only show the consequences of the ongoing ecological destruction, but also remind us of our animal nature, our non-privileged status within the network of life.

It has been long known that human beings are deeply involved in the relations with other species from both a biological and a coevolutionary point of view, especially since the domestication of the great herbivores starting from the Neolithic, in the Fertile Crescent, which gave rise to closer and closer relations of proximity and cohabitation. It is thought that most infectious pathologic agents are really zoonoses or, better, anthropozoonoses. Measles is perhaps one of the most striking examples of spillover, as it is derived from rinderpest. The passage is believed to have occurred in ancient times, probably in the Middle Ages; what is certain is that the prolonged cohabitation of the human and bovine species in the Old World has given rise to forms of cross-immunity, leading to a human mortality rate of around 0.1%. Unfortunately, this immunity was not present in the populations of the Americas and this has led, for example, in Hawaii, to a mortality rate of one fifth of the population, and in Fiji of almost a third. Veterinary authorities are accustomed to dealing with zoonoses and there is no doubt that, if today people manage to live together with animals such as dogs and cats, this is also due to the development of veterinary medicine and the prophylactic measures taken. For years, however, veterinary institutions have been recommending avoidance of close relations with wild animals, stressing that they should never be placed in contact with areas inhabited by humans. Unfortunately, as research by Sara Grant and Christopher W. Olsen (1999) shows, doctors and veterinarians often have different views on zoonotic risk and communicate very little on this subject (159–163).

Such concerns are certainly missing in Asian wet markets, where the circulation of wild or exotic species, whose consumption is very common, creates ideal conditions for the development of zoonoses. A wet market is a place where organic products are sold: mainly fresh meat and fish, but also live animals that are kept in tiny cages, to be slaughtered on the spot or sold directly to buyers. These are veritable circles of hell, where a large number of risk factors converge, such as: i) situations of serious ill-treatment of animals, well beyond the limit of torture, for food uses passed off as delicacies, which obviously predispose them to infections; ii) lack of the most basic health and hygiene standards, with feces, blood and all kinds of contaminants suspended in the air and in the form of slurry; (iii) appalling epidemiological promiscuity, not only because of the lack of adequate space between animals, but also because of the presence of wild animals in the midst of domestic varieties and the high proportion of animals from other geographical areas. In wet markets we find fish, birds of all kinds, pigs, dogs, raccoons, pangolins, bats, porcupines and snakes, just to give a few examples. Leaving aside for a moment the ethical aspect, we can ask ourselves why these forms of trade even exist, when it is well known that great pandemics always originate from the carelessness of our interactions with other species, from an epidemiological and an ecological point of view. Unfortunately, the answer lies in cultural roots which concern food, consumerism, traditional medicine and purchasing habits. Also, a non-secondary contributing factor is the attraction that these places arouse in Western tourists (Sanchez 2019; Guppy 2020).

This account of zoonoses therefore goes hand in hand with what has been said about our ecological relations with other species. There are many links between animals: considering different species as separate entities does not allow us to understand the health dynamics that ultimately concern us. There is no doubt that there is considerable literature on the zoonotic emergencies that have affected human beings in recent years. The HIV virus (Human Immunodeficiency Virus), for example, a retrovirus transmissible through organic fluids, originated from a spillover contracted by monkeys, most likely in the hunting and trading of primate meat and skins. Another case of zoonosis was the Ebola infection, whose first epidemic appeared in Zaire in 1976 and then in Sudan, caused by a virus of the Filoviridae family: its reservoirs are probably the fruit bats of Central Africa, whence the virus spilt over into human beings and other primates as its final hosts. The Sars epidemic, linked to the Sars-CoV coronavirus, which first appeared in 2002, is the result of passages between bats and civets which occurred, it is thought, in the wet markets of the Guangdong province.

The current pandemic, linked to the Sars-CoV2 coronavirus, is also the result of a spillover attributable to bats (*Rhinolophus affinis*) and probably to pangolins (Mallapaty 2020), which likely occurred in Hubei province and emerged in the Wuhan market. Zoonoses remind us of the epidemiological link that binds the living, due to the mutagenic capacity of viruses that makes them adaptable to new hosts. The coronavirus family has numerous strains that infect many species of animals, using spike proteins that attach themselves to the cellular receptors of the host in a selective way; these molecules give the virus a crownlike appearance. In the case of the human being, Covid-19 infects the cells, interacting with particular receptors called ACE2, an affinity that seems to be present also in cats and ferrets. Immunity should therefore neutralize these bonding proteins. Interesting ongoing research, presented in the journal *Microbes and Infection* by researchers Bruno Tilocca and Paola Roncada (2020), hypothesizes that previous contact with dogs infected with specific coronavirus can exert protection against human Covid-19, due to the high level of homology between the two strains in spike protein epitopes. This would be a case of cross-immunity, which again demonstrates that the interspecific epidemiological relationship is much more complex than one might think.

Certainly, places such as wet markets represent ideal settings for cases of spillover while not encouraging any processes of cross-immunization, which require longer periods of time in which different species coexist. On the other hand, there are also other phenomena that can favor dangerous spillovers. The massive destruction of entire ecosystems, with the result of forcing millions of animals to move, especially those with wings such as bats and birds, breaks the delicate balance between pathogens, creating a situation of great danger. The construction of intensive breeding farms, with millions of poultry or pigs, often in places where wild species previously resided, favors dangerous epidemic triangulations, with connections from wild to domestic animals. The latter – due to the high number of individual, who are also highly stressed and therefore more exposed to contagion – act as a sounding board for the acquisition of virulence factors and successful transition to human beings. The tendency to market wild animals, for the most varied reasons, determines interactions for which our immune system is not prepared.

On the other hand, it must be said that even the relationship between domesticated varieties and wild species is not always as confinable as one would like, so a wild population can become a reservoir of infection for domesticated animals and vice versa, with dangerous spillovers that place humans at the center. Nowadays, for example, there is concern about the possible contagion of African swine fever in the relationship between the population of wild boar and domestic pigs. The clearest example of this process is that of bird flu infections due to orthomyxovirus, whose reservoirs are wild birds – especially aquatic species – capable of transmitting the infection to farmed poultry through feces. This way, domesticated birds become the first intermediate passageway, whilst pigs would be the second, as they have receptors both for avian and human viruses, thus playing the role of incubators and then of contagion triggers in relation to our species. It is to be noted that over the last few years we have also seen frequent passages of avian flu to other mammals, especially in zoos. Finally, in the 1990s it was possible to demonstrate direct contagion between poultry on the one hand and people, dogs and cats on the other, with a considerable diffusive and pandemic risk, due to the high mutation index characterizing influenza viruses by antigenic drift or shift, through recombination or hybridization with other human influenza viruses.

The analysis of the H1N1 influenza virus – associated with the Spanish flu that killed tens of millions of people around the world a hundred years ago – found that all eight genetic segments are derived from an avian virus adapted by spillover. As reported by Quammen: Spanish flu "had its ultimate source in a wild aquatic bird, and after passing through some combination of domesticated animals [. . .] emerged to kill as many as 50 million people before receding into obscurity" (2020: 22). The problem with zoonoses contracted from wild animals, either directly or through an amplifying host found in domestic animals, shows us a set of risks that require increasing epidemiological attention. On the one hand, it is important to stress the necessity of preserving ecosystems, given that within the niche cycle each virus coexists with other living forms without doing substantial damage. On the other hand, it asks us to raise our guard when it comes to pets, combating opportunities for promiscuity and increasing veterinary supervision, as well as avoiding the overcrowding we have seen with the emergence of intensive animal breeding. It is also necessary to have a different socio-cultural approach to the problem, involving: i) anthropologists, to understand how populations have developed cultures of coexistence with wild animals and collect experiences to deal with potential problems; ii) sociologists, to reflect on how changes in demographic dynamics and human mobility can increase epidemic risk parameters.

To sum up, the factor that currently contributes most to the emergence of new zoonoses is the increasing impact of human beings on wild environments, caused by several factors: i) the conversion of ecosystems into agronomic areas with increased contact between humans and animals that are resistant to them; ii) the destruction of habitats, in terms of the resources available to wild animals and their areas for shelter and breeding, with the consequent displacement of these animals into human areas; iii) the use of wild animals imported or sold in markets of large conurbations, as in the case of Wuhan; iv) the transfer of allochthonous species to new environments, giving rise to pathogen exchanges between wildlife; v) the transport of exotic fauna from one continent to another;

vi) the implementation of intensive breeding in natural habitats. In the last-mentioned case, the most perfect of spillover triangulations is achieved: the passage from wild to domestic animals and from the latter to human beings. An example of this was the emergence of the Nipah virus in Malaysia in the late 1990s, when an intensive pig farm was set up in the habitat of fruit bats that were reservoirs of the virus. The massive pig population acted as a viral amplifier, causing a contagion that was contained in that case, but which showcases the evolution of such infectious events.

We can then ask why birds and bats are so often vectors of viral infections and why pigs and poultry are most often directly involved in the transmission to humans. While bats represent the largest group of mammals in this class, and avian species are great epidemiological mixing vessels, the most trivial but perhaps most plausible answer is that both have great mobility, especially when they are deprived of their niche ecosystems. This should also give rise to reflection on human behavior. As regards the second question, it is clear that the large number of animals stocked in pig and poultry farms makes the virulence of any disease very likely. Even in viral infections, there are adaptive developments that has taken place over long periods of time, since in order to remain present a pathogen must create a balanced relationship with its host, causing a chronic infection and using the individual as a point of passage for a new host. The severity of the pandemics we are facing today is linked to the fact that, by altering these balances, we accidentally became the victims, like a fire that has no safety barrier in front of it.

The increase in meat consumption in Western countries and in other countries such as China and Japan, which has characterized the last fifty years, has not only had serious ecological consequences, as mentioned, but has also led to very dangerous epidemiological situations. In order to satisfy a demand that was growing at an exponential rate, supported by the false equivalence between welfare and the availability of animal products on the table, intensive farms have been set up capable of housing thousands of animals, subject to a weight or productivity increase regime – think of the batteries of laying hens or dairy cows – which has stretched any physiological limit. This could be done through many interventions: genetic selection based on breeds; the massive use of drugs able to promote productive conversion or to support debilitated animals; a diet based on hyper-proteic regimes even with the use of meat flour; and the architectural transformation of structures that look more and more like laagers. Since the 1980s there has been a succession of health emergencies to be extinguished through the massive slaughter of animals (stamping out), with phenomena that worry public opinion such as mad cow disease (Marchesini 1996b). When we point the finger at the malpractice of the Chinese wet markets, we must not forget that horrors and high-risk epidemiological conditions are also found in the West – the only difference is that they occur behind the closed walls of the sheds.

3 The Technological Virus

3.1 Premise

What we have left behind is a time without history or, better, a time that we claimed to set onto a variable "k", without direction (Prigogine & Stengers 1979), which can be subtracted from the narrative key. In our wish to eliminate its texture, reducing it to a homogeneous factor devoid of thermodynamic resistances, it was as if time had disappeared from our lives. And now, suddenly, it presents itself to us in its most disturbing guise. We thought we could do without its specific value, as if every event of life could be treated as an algorithm (Dennett 2004), so we ignored the historical reports about the organization of the network of life, thus triggering the ecological and epidemiological problems in place. To think inside the connections means, on the contrary, to admit a historical interdependence of human beings in the biosphere and to acknowledge the irreversibility of processes: therefore, it means rejecting the view from the outside.

The voices that rose up in the past century to focus on environmental issues have not been heard or at least have not affected the development model and the habits of people (Passmore 1974; Midgley 1978). Perhaps this is because the deontological call to defend nature alone does not make up for a lack of childhood ties with the biosphere, or for the time we have not spent in a direct relationship with ecological dynamics. If only we go back a few generations we discover a bond, certainly not supported by ethical considerations but, nevertheless, rooted in people because it is supported by early memories, vivid emotions, sensory resonances and rhythms acquired from childhood. Now we discover that without that bond there is no responsiveness, because there is no nostalgia, that is, that feeling that binds everyone to their own Ithaca, that fills something with value that is not payable but felt, because the nostalgic responsiveness (Emerson 1836; Schopenhauer 1851; Morreale 2009) continuously reminds us that something is missing, that a root of experience has been severed.

The time gone by speaks to us of something else and now we lack references; we say that everything will change, but haven't got the slightest idea how: we lack perspective. We have spent too much time locked inside our magic boxes – televisions, tablets, mobile phones, accessing at any time any TV series, Disney fantasies, Marvel superheroes, electronic games and social media – in a constant connection always hungry for more electromagnetic waves, chasing a chimerical purely human dimension (Augé 1999). And this need for distraction, the compulsion to be, in fact, disjoint from the world, made us bulimic consumers of technology, in a sort of techno-addiction (Demichelis 2018) freed from the imperatives that had characterized the twentieth century. Whereas in the past, there was a claim that technology would free people's time, lighten their work, and speed up their practices, the drive to consume technology in recent decades has been characterized by the need to occupy people's time, to converge their nonworking moments into a collective intoxication of images.

This being immersed in the infosphere was, after all, a tendency already accredited in collective practice, sometimes subject to the fierce criticism of traditionalists for giving visibility to the most degrading expressions of people, other times hailed as an opportunity for easier interaction. People complained that Facebook encouraged verbal bullying (Manca & Petrone 2014; Pennetta 2019) by so-called cyberbullies, that Instagram could favor the publication of private images on the net, that the flourishing of pornographic sites stimulated the phenomenon of pedophilia or that easy access to videogames was creating addictions, or else that the increase in online betting worsened the phenomenon of ludopathy. The connection-addiction disease was already interpreted as an infection, contracted from a virus that increasingly broadened the front of contagion, affecting people differently by age groups.

The elderly population is the most critical in the face of the risk of techno-addiction and the most sensitive to individual freedoms, as they still remember the struggles after World War II. The loss of part of their freedom thus seems to translate the two forms of infection in an epidemiological sense. Conspiracy theories deserve irony, but at the same time they express a long-standing climate of suspicion towards power and the institutions, as well as the popular view that behind any major event there is a hidden agenda (McConnachie & Tudge 2005; Ciuffoletti 1993) rather than a domino effect of out-of-control problems. Everything, then, seems to converge into a coherent plan: locking people down to act undisturbed, creating a virus to rid society of its last resistance to the digital revolution, etc. Unlike the morbidity of coronavirus, which wipes out people over 70, in the case of new forms of virtual connection it is the youngest who are first infected by the technomedia epidemic, an example of this being the phenomenon of social media.

Life at the time of coronavirus resumes and makes explicit a process that had already been inaugurated in the cyberpunk imagination of the 1980s. As in William Gibson's story *Burning Chrome* (1982), cyberspace has become the epic stage of individual agency, the new frontier and postmodern Troy for the use and consumption of every hero. Information technologies have, therefore, allowed the construction of participation models which are very different from the community ones, isolating people further in the paradox of an easier connection. Similar to an epidemic, it has affected the groups most susceptible to viral proteins, conquering them like a population without immunity.

The virus model can thus be useful to understand some aspects of the interaction between the individual and technology, abandoning the anthropo-centric idea whereby human beings are completely in control of the techno-scientific upheavals that occur. Obviously I am not saying that technology is a virus, but rather that the relationship we have with technology has aspects of reciprocity, that is, feedback on the human being, which are often ignored.

3.2 The Technological Infection

Interpreting technological upheavals in an epidemiological way allows us to understand how every event that inaugurates a new performance, made possible by a technology or a technique (technomediation), has both emergence and morbidity effects. In fact, this phenomenon has unpredictable outcomes because the body is transformed by the encounter with it, and in this metamorphosis effects arise that can only be evaluated ex-post (Greenfield 2015: 189–208). For other aspects we must speak of morbidity because of the vulnerability it causes in the human being, requiring time for an immune rebalancing (Esposito 2011). Technologies have undoubtedly enabled humans to achieve very high-profile goals, helping them overcome major challenges in scientific research, medicine, transport and communication, just to name a few examples. At the same time, though, it is clear that the development of an impressive technological apparatus has made human beings both increasingly dependent on this resource and increasingly exposed to profound transformations in their life context, which sometimes is not easy to manage.

The advent of mass media has built a new type of society – I refer to the points made, for example, by Umberto Eco (2016) – because it changed the order of contact between people, just as the digital revolution has given rise to new forms of contagion for which we were not prepared. Social media have revolutionized the communicative style, above all of the youngest people, inaugurating new forms of accreditation, affiliation, visibility and marketing. Interconnection does not only allow us to expand our range of interaction, but also produces undesirable effects, such as: i) the intrusion of hackers into private spaces, bank accounts or databases; ii) putting our work equipment at risk of computer viruses; iii) allowing strangers to activate our computer's webcam and spy on us. However, I think that it is wrong to focus only on the problems that can be generically referred to the Web, because, in fact, there are countless advantages and opportunities that have come with it. This is not, therefore, my intention.

What I want to say is that the advent of digitization, as an experiential prevalence, has radically transformed our relational life, exposing us to external factors of influence that require new forms of immunity.

Using the virus as a metaphor can be helpful to understand the infection-like effects that we sometimes see with the advent of new technologies, which seem to penetrate the human being, just like a virus entering a cell, to reprogram its functions. In these cases, we witness consequences that can no longer be interpreted as simple performative enhancements or extensions, as Marshall McLuhan's (1964) interpretation has accustomed us to do. I therefore believe it is important to adopt a systemic approach to the interpretation of *techne* – in other words, an ecological methodology that is able to call into question the juxtaposition view. The traditional interpretation has relegated the instrument to the role of a passive entity at the service of human purposes, always external to the body and therefore never able to hybridize it. The humanistic reading sees technology as a sort of crutch or compensation for a deficit of human nature (Marchesini 2017: 9–15), a sort of external guardian unable to operate beyond the functional categories of subsidiarity.

Today, with the advent of intradermal chips and biotechnologies, we discover that this vision is very limited, because it is increasingly clear that computer and genetic engineering interfaces are not only able to bypass our decision-making functions and to dialogue directly with the operational bases of our physiology, but can also enter the body and modify its functional organization. This of course leads to profound shifts in meaning, but the point is not to focus on the advent of the latest technologies, but to rethink the interaction between body and technology at its root (Gourhan 1945; Rivoltella & Rossi 2019: 51–67; Simondon 1958), through an interpretation of functional co-factoriality. In this view, the instrument also plays an active role in the human system, not only enabling previously impossible performances, but also transforming our way of being in the world in all aspects, even in terms of the goals we set ourselves.

Each relationship produces a transformation of the intersection categories, so that the relationship with technology, too, makes humans less closed off within their species dimension, operating a sort of decentralization and creating greater exposure to external influences. Technology has helped human beings to better understand the behavior of other species, both through digital simulations, neuroimaging tools, equipment able to provide us with reports on sensory systems different from ours and by highlighting the bias inherent in our own *Umwelt* (von Uexküll 2010).

This means, for example, that the instrument does more than just enhance a function and remain outside the body, acting as a servant of human purposes, conceived as autonomous and referable only to free and rational decisions. Technology rather transforms our perspective on the world, making new needs emerge, establishing new evaluation parameters for the standards of functional effectiveness and efficiency, creating dependencies in all aspects of our life, and setting new goals and expectations. What falls apart is thus the assumption of the fullness of human governance regarding the use of technology, which represents one of the most deeply rooted legacies of modernity. The humanist tradition has interpreted *techne* as compensation or reparation for a human nature considered deficient and incomplete, which therefore had to appeal to external means in order to ensure survival.

On closer inspection, though, neither does the hypothesis of the incompleteness of human nature (Gehlen 1940) hold up from a descriptive point of view – that is giving a detailed account of the anatomical and physiological characteristics of our species, on the contrary, highlights the complexity and niche specialization of hominids: the perception of performative insufficiency of the body is the effect of an a posteriori evaluation of technomediation. That is, it is nothing more than an explanatory bias, which leads us to assign a causal valence to a consequence of the process itself. In other words, we can say that the advent of a technology is not caused by a somatic deficiency to be compensated, but rather produces, as a consequence, a feeling of deficiency. It is the same as falling in love: it is only as a result of it that we miss our partner, not prior to it. Similarly, the advent of the mobile phone made us dependent on it, so today we feel naked if we are deprived of its reassuring presence and we fall into panic if the battery runs out or if there is no signal, while in the 1970s we lived perfectly well even without it. A technology, in fact, modifies the bar of performance standards – not only enhancing them, but also transforming them – so that, once accustomed, we feel deprived of our own prerogatives at the mere idea of doing without that medium.

The relationship with technology has a significant impact on the somatic structure through some particular actions because: i) it inaugurates a different priority of functions, often changing the game of relevant factors, (think for example of the importance of the response function in digital games); ii) it changes the type of performance required, giving one person more chances of success than another; iii) it changes the way in which different functions are performed, for example the use of hands when typing on a smartphone; iv) by acting as a development environment, it produces growth differentials by exercise, because an organ develops on the basis of the exercise it performs, thus changing the body's weight balances. This is why the metaphor of the virus, which penetrates the cell and reconfigures it according to its functional logic, can be useful to understand how technology modifies the body and does not simply serve it.

Technology acts on all systems, especially the endocrine (Ikemoto & Panksepp 1999: 6–41), immune (Afifi et al. 2018: 265–273) and neurobiological (Dehaene 2019: 193–194) systems, so that a boy growing up in a constant relationship with a computer configures his PNEI (psycho-neuro-endocrine-immunology) system in a very different way from a non-digital native (Haughton, Aiken & Cheevers 2015: 504–518). Technology is somatized, acting exactly like a virus. We can see, for example, how practices have changed with the advent of the smartphone: consider, for instance, the use of two thumbs instead of the grip. However, this is only the tip of the iceberg because, as Derrick de Kerckhove (1991) suggested, each technology produces a brain frame and has an impact on the whole organism. Screen light changes the epiphyseal function with alterations in the wake–sleep rhythm (Brainard et al. 2001: 6405–6412; Higuchi et al. 2014: 3298–3303); the prevalence of response speed in electronic games, producing a spread of arousal, alters the adrenal function (Nikkelen 2014: 2228–2241) and decreases the ability to concentrate; pancreatic endocrine functions are also altered, with alterations in the glucose cycle and metabolism.

Also, keeping still in front of a monitor reduces the production of endorphins, which we know are related to muscle function, emphasizing states of anxiety and sensitivity; at the same time, more contained physical effort reduces serotonergic function, exposing us to feelings of dissatisfaction. The same motor reduction lowers the functionality of the immune system which, deprived of its own pump, relies on that of muscle contraction; likewise, spending less time in the open air reduces the synthesis of vitamin D, further lowering the body's defenses. It's becoming increasingly evident that technology is changing us, reducing certain cognitive faculties, such as memory. The habit of spending a good part of the day watching a screen induces a posture that bends the neck forward, modifying the spinal column and consequently the cervical sensitivity (Jacobs & Baker 2002: 221–226). Sexuality is also undergoing relevant transformations, favoring forms of passivity, autoerotism and the consumption of pornographic material, based on simplified evocations and computerized hyper-real images. The body thus adapts to the new environment and this has effects on the ontogenetic process that can no longer be ignored, not to mention the epigenetic alterations – which have not yet been taken into account but which undoubtedly may arise – and, in the long term, the shift in selective pressures.

By increasing the human capacity to act, technology also changes our view of the world. In fact, as the philosopher Hans Jonas points out in *The Imperative of Responsibility* (1984), every extension of the human being's operational field produces new horizons of responsibility. It then becomes problematic to strictly separate facts from values. The principle of naturalistic fallacy, enunciated by

David Hume, affirms that facts do not descend from values and vice versa. However, in view of the above, it is equally problematic to rule out the possibility that there are no intersections between facts and values. It is, in fact, evident that science and ethics are linked together in a problematic relationship, that is, that every technoscientific event produces problems for ethics, and likewise every advance in ethical reflection produces new fields of research for technoscience.

3.3 Technomediation and Exploitation

The idea that through technology humans not only do not affect their own somatic dimension, but even free themselves from ecological dynamics, has reinforced the separative prejudice, on the one hand by increasing the yearning for human domination over the world, on the other hand by transforming the entire biosphere into something to be plundered. How much has the dichotomous conception of nature/culture contributed to strengthening the logic of alienation? In my opinion, a lot. The humanistic understanding of *techne* has favored: i) the development of a mechanistic and alienated vision of nature, providing another shore from which to observe the biosphere; ii) the emancipatory image of humans that underlies the various dualisms drawing the human as a world apart. I am not interested in proposing a sort of neoluddism, a vague and useless return to Walden Pond (Thoreau 1957), because the problem does not concern technomediation itself, but rather the convergence of a feverish technopoietic development into a cultural milieu still rooted in an essentialist conception. This legacy – that is, the interpretative straitjacket that Charles Darwin had to fight against according to the words of Ernst Mayr (1982) – lent itself to reading the technological apparatus as an instrument of power over nature and as a great container able to shelter us from the dangers of the world. Essentialism, if it is not able to understand the relational – ecological – nature of qualities, inevitably tends to maintain a rigid separation or a presumption of extraneousness between the human being and the network of life. At most, it outlines an oleographic vision of nature as an uncontaminated place, one that is not inserted within a world system of which the human being is also part, with its economy and social organization.

The affirmation that living beings are extraneous to each other in their various dimensions – from the epidemiological to the ecological one – has produced a reduction of the biological community to a "cheap resource" (Moore 2014: 285–314). The cultural matrix of the anthropocentric celebration of the human being, as an entity that emancipates itself from the constraints of nature through technology, has transformed us into a disease for the planet. The problem lies, also in this case, in the interpretation given to *techne*: no longer seen as a factor of conjunction, the bearer of innumerable dependencies on the network of life, but as an element of separation. This was undoubtedly the biggest misjudgment that could be made, developing a system that institutionalized the dynamics of violation of otherness through *techne*. The critical issues we have to deal with today were, therefore, already present at the dawning of this society-world, focused on the subjugation of *techne* to the exploitation project. Making it the very expression of power and the armed hand of reification, *techne* was thought of as an instrument rather than an *Umwelt*. The metamorphosis of the system required today is therefore not only about bringing the interpretation of human action back into the biospheric matrix, but also about acquiring a new culture of *techne*.

Technological evolution has not freed humans from their interdependencies, but on the contrary has made them even more closely linked to the dynamics of the living. The cybernetic idealism (Marchesini 2018a: 22–25) which claims today to disjoin the factors involved, extracting them from the network of relations based on the matrix of history, as selfishly replicating memes (Dawkins 1976) without a rooted context, prevents us from understanding the meaning of the crises in progress. This misunderstanding/avoidance is due to the insistence on an anti-historical view by which society is separate from ecology, and the economy is separate from the biosphere. It refers primarily to a reversibility of phenomena that does not take into account the specificities of the biosphere. Time has thus become a metronome that beats the rhythm of world production and digestion, with an absolute lack of attention to the irreversible alterations we are causing on the planet. We are witnessing a process of desertification that can be generally attributed to humanity, and yet people themselves are the first to suffer from ecological crises – just like the rest of the living, they are the elective victims of the contagion.

We are seeing it now. The cuts in healthcare, even in European countries, such as Italy and Spain where universal health care exists, highlights the difficulties in dealing with emergencies in hospitals, due to a lack of beds or mechanical ventilation: it is estimated, for example, that from 1998 to 2017 in Italy the number of hospital beds decreased from 331,000 to 191,000 (source: Istat). And the basic supplies, such as masks and prophylactic clothing for medical and nursing staff, are lacking. On the other hand, the coronavirus emergency situation in the United States, and in all other countries with a for-profit health care system, has shown the failure of the liberalist model, which failed to produce effective safeguards, both in terms of prevention and in terms of readiness to deal with the infection epidemic. Those who pay the highest price for the convergence of epidemiological and economic problems are once again the weakest segments of the population, especially in those countries, such as India, which have more substantial pockets of poverty. Moreover, while it is true that climate change will not respect geographical boundaries of any kind, it is undeniable that the capacity for mobility and for the amortization of discomforts will not be the same for everyone. It is often pointed out that the ecological crisis is showing its further meaning of exploitation of people. Like a viral infection, all kinds of problems are more strongly felt by organisms that are already weakened, so the system must inevitably be considered as a whole.

So what is the role of technology in all this? Perhaps, more coherently, we should ask ourselves what role capitalist interpretation assigns to technomediation. In fact, not only does access to the latest technology produce an operational disparity among human beings, but the subsequent declination in the form of oligopoly accentuates the ability of some potentates to exercise new forms of control and exploitation, through: traceability and profiling, whence the fall of the last remnants of privacy; the development of mass orientation and influence on the media. The democracy of the digital network, just like the free market, is proving to be one of the greatest deceptions in history. Our drunken obsession with technological gadgets makes us forget all that these choices support: from the exploitation of children in cobalt mines to the hellish underground tunnels of coltan, indispensable for smartphones. On the other hand, it is clear that, since the Industrial Revolution, technological choices have progressively moved in the direction of more and more energy-intensive and impactful orientations.

The word "Anthropocene" has become a sort of reading key that, however, struggles to hold up both from the point of view of a simple geological attribution – the idea of a Quaternary Era, cut out on the metric of our species, has already been shown to be a stretch – and with regard to the interpretation of the ongoing ecological crisis. The twentieth century undoubtedly marked a step in technological evolution that cannot be ignored, with the revolution of physics, in theoretical and applicative terms, in the first half of the century and then of biology in the second half.

But where do we start to understand this paradigm, which aims to extract the socioeconomic system from its substratum and from the events of life, with an alchemical practice of purification of the "anthropos" essence? Both in the anthropocentric exaltation and in the anthropogenic attribution of the crisis, the aim is to separate humanity from the world and to make it follow its own dynamics, outside of and sheltered from their historical roots. In my opinion, this is a legacy that has widespread philosophical roots, but which has found its accelerator in the modern age. The Cartesian formula of ontological introflection – that is, putting the consistency of the world in brackets – can be considered the founding principle of the extraction of humanity from the network of economic and ecological interdependencies of the living. Hence also the transformation of the nonhuman universe into a "cheap resource." This separation of economic and social dynamics from the network of life has determined the claim to consider the two domains, the economic domain of human beings and the ecological domain of the nonhuman, as separate. This is the interpretative error known as "human exceptionalism" (Smith 2002), which is the basis of many of the processes of reification, marginalization and exploitation occurring in the present planetary crisis. The whole system must be framed in its historical dimension and, therefore, cannot be dismissed as a purely ecological-descriptive aspect.

As rightly remarked by Jason W. Moore (2016), the attribution of the problem to a generic entity defined as "anthropos" – that is, the act of bringing the etiology back to an anthropogenic factor, without entering into the specifics of a system which involves power, capital and the biosphere – risks functioning as a mask so as not to go into the examination of the real critical factors. In Moore's preface to the Italian edition of his book *Anthropocene or Capitalocene? Nature, History, and the Crisis of Capitalism* (2017) we read: "Climate change is not the result of human action in the abstract sense, but the most obvious consequence of centuries of dominance of capital." Undoubtedly, moreover, the exploitation of resources does not exclusively concern capitalist systems, and this leads us to reflect on how modernity has taken the path of the massive exploitation of nature.

Technology has been conceived on account of a culture based on the exploitation of nature, in an anthropocentric logic, and without attention to the energy-intensive character of human activities. We therefore need a new culture of *techne*, able to help human beings change their perspective on the world and to be more attentive to the decrease in consumption and the reduction of pollutants. We therefore need to rethink the system rather than simply reconsider ecology, which alone cannot overcome the assumptions of a socio-economic matrix that is detached from the biosphere and still rooted within separations established in the modern age.

In order to examine how the ecological problem has been misled by the dualisms underlying the independence of human socioeconomic dynamics from the network of life, it is essential to think about the enucleative principles, that is the viral logic that has sought to transform our species into an entity with no metabolism of interdependence. This has made it possible to set up mechanisms of infection aimed at every type of otherness, so that the body of the other has been transformed into flesh to be used outside of any integrative mechanism: a "body without organs" (Deleuze & Guattari 1978–1980; Marchesini 2020) to be exploited for a replicative benefit, only to abandon it like a worn-out corpse. The virus metaphor is therefore effective to show us a model of self-representation that has created a global system, based on a certain culture of *techne*, where the prevailing dynamics are not accidentally negligent with respect to natural resources, but constitutionally based on exploitation. The viral paradigm therefore lies in thinking of otherness as a resource and technology as a tool that makes it available cheaply, instead of recognizing ourselves as part of the network.

3.4 Cybernetic Idealism

Our relationship with technology has changed profoundly in recent decades due to two major revolutions, the biotechnological and the digital, which have in many ways volatilized our reality, lowering its material and stability roots. Let me explain this better. When an instrument is conceived in an analogical way it adheres to a very specific substratum, because vinyl is something different from the paper of a book or a photographic film. We could say that reading a book is in some way related to the tactile relationship with paper, just as listening to a piece of music is linked to the whole liturgy of the vinyl. Likewise, beyond the film, which in itself is rich in quality, photography also recalls the darkroom with its red light and the sour smell of acids. These are experiences that create a consubstantiality of the experiences of reading, music and image with the materials that allow access to them.

This makes them different worlds because they are connected to different interface materials, with which one must necessarily interact. The digitalization of these accesses disconnects the experience from the medium, we could say that it dematerializes it, connecting the subject no longer to an instrument but to an infosphere, capable of transferring the sole sensory content of the experience: the sound and the image. We thus get used to navigating within a reality that can do without matter, a reality dominated by the volatility of the sensory element (McQuivey 2013; Marchesini 2018b). While the relationship with an object, be it a vinyl record or a film, indicates the "embodied" presence of the sensory experience we wish to have, in its digital translation it presents itself as a viral entity that does not need to permanently reside in a body that supports it.

The analogical world is therefore made of objects, of indissoluble relationships between the sensory elements – or, if you like, the function-experience they make possible – and the matter that gives expression to it. Instead, the digital world is linked to fragments of binary information, that is to say, to strings of data that run on the hardware. In this regard, the virus metaphor can be useful to understand the volatility of digital content. The hardware enables its processing, but does not correspond to intrinsic qualities of the medium – such as those of vinyl or film – that is, these qualities do not reside in it. Information can travel from one container to another because it is, in fact, free from the predicates of the substrate, more referable to an infectious process than to a substantialist expression of matter. This leads to a second important shift: the fall of the essentialism of the instruments. Being inextricably bound to a given material made the different function-experience worlds separate from each other, incapable of dialogue and above all not hybridizable and not convertible.

This was lost with the digital revolution, which transformed every instrument in the same logic of the binary code, creating instead of or next to the experiential workshop, a second infospheric dimension. The digital experience can be accessed by immersion and not simply by grasping an object, such as a book or a photo album, which is proposed as a disjointed item and still leaves you in the room. The tools that produce the function – be they the camera or the turntable – or contain it, that is, the photograph and the record, are dematerialized and at the same time deprived of their essential qualities to dissolve in the infectious continuum. The metamorphosis is deep, because people who have grown up since the 1990s, the so-called digital natives, have lost the habit of dealing with objects endowed with intrinsic qualities, which can be manipulated according to specific practices (Wilen 2018), assuming an immersive style with a prevalence of sensoriality.

Science fiction has completed this process of dematerialization of experience by also applying the virus paradigm to the mind, that is, the idea of transferability or volatility of the brain. Thinking of the mind as a packet of data that happens to run on the hardware that nature has given us, but that precisely because of their viral consistency could be released from the flesh to be digitized, has given life to all the fantastic narratives of recent decades: from time travel to memory grafts, from downloading on silicon media to the idea of eternal life. Cartesian dualism thus presents itself in an immanent key, replacing *res cogitans* with *res informatica*, and it is no coincidence that one of the cult films of the late twentieth century, *Matrix* by the Wachowski sisters, takes up the idea of the French philosopher and translates it into a reality invented through neurosimulation. Thinking of one's mind as a sort of transferable and replicable supersoftware is to all intents and purposes equivalent to thinking of oneself as a virus.

This also means projecting oneself into a dimension other than the realm of the organic. Such a view goes further than the myth of the inorganic developed in the twentieth century: from the futuristic celebration of the machine to the "sex appeal of the inorganic" theorized by the Italian philosopher Mario Perniola (1994), this myth had impregnated the daily life of the middle class with fetishism. What is dominating now, instead, is a sort of cybernetic idealism that dreams of the immaterial and seeks residence within the data flow of the web. New forms of sublimation are opening up. It is no coincidence that Wally Pfister titled *Transcendence* (2014) the story of a scientist whose consciousness is uploaded into a computer and then connected to the internet. Beyond the science fiction aspect, this film also reveals a collective imagination that is increasingly oriented towards a cybernetic perception of the Self, resulting in dwelling aspirations and roots that are far from adhering to the network of life. But alongside the cinematic suggestion, such an attitude is a litmus test of customary habits already in existence.

The digital transformation, in short, has radically changed our relationship with the media. It has created, to all intents and purposes, a second reality – the "infospheric" one, inside which people seem more and more like prisoners. People, especially the younger generations, are totally unprepared for this kind of captivity. The "hikikomori" (Ismail 2018; Ricci 2008) phenomenon seems to be an infection of the spirit, which shows the inability of young people to live a convivial life, preferring to shut themselves away in a virtual world. The stormy and uncontrolled development of social media leaves people totally exposed to the infection of media viruses, which destroy critical capacity with respect to information, models and styles, so that what matters is no longer competence but visibility, and there is no longer any difference between a valid piece of information from an accredited source and the mere replication of random content. Today more than ever, technology shows its infiltrative character by somatizing itself, and this metamorphosis requires a profound change of perspective.

4 The Return of the Body

4.1 Premise

If one adopts as a model the volatility of a virus, its passage through the world without taking root and its high mutability index, one can come to imagine that even the body is a liquid entity that can be changed with extreme ease, through forms of cosmetic surgery and performative doping, and that – why not? – can be abandoned altogether to move into some other somatic garment. The trans-humanist movement (Drexler 1986; Kurzweil 2005), like the well-known science-fiction narrative, paints the body as a container to be modified at will or possibly discarded for a better one. For some authors even the mind, as a biographical whole, can be interpreted as a package of information that can be transferred from the brain to another medium: the "mind uploading" project is perhaps the most explicit expression of this view (Paul & Cox 1996; Doyle 1996). And this is no secondary aspect, because it is based on how we think about being-a-body that we construct our existential dimension and our relationship with nature. We thus claim to defend other species, ecosystems and future generations, yet we are unable to recognize our own being rooted in a body, which in turn is interconnected with the biosphere.

The dynamics of a virus is simple and clear – at least that is how it can appear (Hurst 2000: 11–33; Malmstrom 2018) – in its treatment of the body as a sort of Petri dish (breeding ground) for replication. In fact, it is so simple that today it is proposed as a paradigm of new forms of existential nomadism. The theme of the invaded body recurs often in the modern age, and in many ways it has provided us with a key to interpreting various phenomena, such as Descartes' *res cogitans* or Richard Dawkins' memes. Images of the parasite that takes possession of the body and bends it for its own purposes – like a computer virus that invades the memory of a device or alters its processes, or a psychotropic ideology that blinds reasoning – are recurrences that can be brought back to the same conceptual archetype. It is this dualist approach that prevents any true ecological thinking and distances us from a systemic logic able to treat phenomena as emergences of co-factoriality, as non-linear recursive processes and, finally, as state functions.

The virus paradigm thus becomes a model that lends itself to transmit the concept of "inhabiting the body", which presupposes not recognizing oneself, except in part, in one's own flesh. Computer science, through the combination of hardware and software, has strengthened this image, so that in the second half of the twentieth century the mind was conceived and described as a virus that infects or runs on the neurobiological computer. According to Daniel Dennett, a person is nothing more than a hominid infected by cultural symbionts (2003: 228).

The exposure of flesh to contagion – in addition to bringing with it the body's reduction to a simple substratum and supporting old dichotomies in a new guise – stigmatizes its weakness, leads it back to the paternalistic dialectic of the female form as a receptacle, and finally transforms physicality into a consumer good. Meat becomes the product *par excellence*, to the point that in the West it also represents the ultimate meal, transforming every other form of food into a side dish. Flesh is the product of the pornographic market: it can become a canvas, such as in body art (Alfano Miglietti 2008); it supports new forms of colonialism through the trade of organs (Adams 2015; Lundin 2015; Scheper-Hughes 2000: 191–224); and it dictates the rules of social and political choices.

So, the body is translated into flesh that is vulnerable to the multiple forms of contagion present in the world: from the media – which according to Byung-

Chul Han (2015) produce real psycho-infections, feeding a sort of self-exploitation of the individual in the West – to technological ones, with the hybrid physiology of the cyborg or the telematic control that enables tracing a person's every expression. The exposure of flesh is the most powerful image of the bewilderment that people are feeling during the pandemic: from the bodies burned in the streets of Guayaquil, Ecuador, to the mass graves on Hart Island, not far from the financial heart of Manhattan. Suddenly we feel the body rebel, coming back to remind us of the error of dualism. Suddenly we hear the deep beat of our animal flesh that throbs with joy or fear, living in a here and now which becomes important and deep, eternal in its minuteness precisely because it is ecologically nested in time and space. So we discover that the future could be different, that the continuum of our certainties is not so obvious after all, that our many impalpable and viral assumptions – the market, the technosphere, progress – will not be able to contain the coming crises.

Today we are talking about SARS-CoV2, but we have to be aware that the future may hold other pandemics for us, because we have forced the homeostatic cycles of the biosphere and we will pay the price for it. Moreover, one can identify many convergences between climatic alterations and the development of epidemics for which we are not prepared: for example, the dissolution of permafrost can put back into circulation paleo-viruses that have been dormant for millions of years (Doucleff 2018; Sirucek 2014). Another source of risk may be xenotransplantation, that is, the use of transgenic pig organs to be transplanted into human beings, with the risk of releasing retroviruses inserted into the pig's genetic heritage (proviruses) that could trigger dangerous infections (Kimsa et al. 2014: 2062–2083). The more viral expressions will appear in the theatre of our lives, the more we will rediscover the sense of being a body, along with the ecological dimension of our presence in the world.

4.2 The Protagonism of the Body

Body, thanks to a pandemic accident, has returned to the center of our reflections. The pandemic is a fear that spreads over all the expressions of the body: over murmurs coming up from the lungs, over a possible photophobia or some warmth around the temples. Never before have we felt like a body, feeling the inconsistencies or, if you like, the insufficiencies of the virtual relationships we are forced to have. Our body is thus reclaiming a role that we had taken for granted, and even the social dimension is taking on the aspect of an issue that concerns the body and the relationship between bodies.

Social distancing is an exemplary means to show the limits of virtual interaction, bringing back the nostalgia of physical contact or even of meeting in person, that pleasure of being in front of each other in all sensory aspects (Books et al. 2020: 912–920). At the same time, it made clear how the various digital communications we were used to were mainly incentives or reminders for appointments in the real world, so that now such technomediated interactions seem to us meaningless suspensions, unable to fill the void we feel. There is a proliferation of research that shows how lockdown has produced significant psychological damage, becoming an enormous experiment of worldwide scope (Van Hoof 2020). But it is not only a question of taking stock of the mental disorders of this epidemiological crisis, but rather of reflecting on the metamorphosis of the perception of the body and of one's relationship with the body. It is our image of the Self that has changed suddenly and radically.

There is no doubt, then, that the advent of the pandemic – because of the prescriptive effect of social isolation, but not only that – sanctioned an overwhelming return of the body, which brought people's attention back within the perimeter of animality. We have a sort of nostalgia for the body, for that carnal expression that is manifested in a tactile and visceral way in being in the world and in contact with others. We miss the bodily expression that finds relief in muscular effort and in its endorphin feedback – in giving voice, in general, to our biological phenomenology. We are indebted to oxytocin, that hormone that is released in an embrace and in the comfort of a caress, and we pay a very high price in terms of anxiety and restlessness when we are deprived of it. This problem is obscured by the prevailing focus on epidemiological and economic issues, and yet it is present, as pointed out by many psychologists and psychiatrists (World Health Organization).

Accustomed to considering the body as a garment to display, while remaining alien to it – a container, to use the concept expressed in Nicole Jones-Dion's *Stasis* (2017) – we struggle to find meaning in the here and now of limbs disconnected from our daily work, in the suspended time we are living. The reasons of the body bring to the surface the incongruities of the nonsense that has been spouted about web-based transcendence. It is not enough, then, to have a new ecological awareness, which reaffirms the importance of dealing with environmental resources in the logic of development or which urges us to protect our ecosystems in order to avoid meteorological or epidemiological disasters: first of all, it is indispensable to fully change the ontological coordinates with which we read our presence as biological entities, "living next to other forms of life" to follow Slavoj Žižek's book *Virus* (2020: 43). We now turn to that same body we had forgotten in our intoxication of techno-mediated nomadism. Biology takes its revenge, highlighting a shift of thought that was already latent in recent decades, marking a break with the approach in vogue in the previous century.

In the twentieth century, in fact, the view of biological processes was based on a genocentric vision, understandable if we consider the large number of discoveries and applications that had followed one another, from James Watson and Francis Crick's 1953 model to the Human Genome Project, completed in April 2003. This vision is how Richard Dawkins presented it in his famous *The Selfish Gene* (1976). The author did nothing but take to extremes the central dogma of molecular biology established in the twentieth century (Crick 1970), according to which there is a "unidirectionality" in the passage of information, from DNA to proteins. In this sense, it was the genetic inheritance that superintended the phenotypic formation of the organism, and this was also the case from a phylogenetic point of view, since the body was believed to be nothing more than a passive container of replicators, the only true actors of the evolutionary process. The body underwent "the infection of the gene" without being able to influence it at all; therefore the protein was under the domain of genes, in a way similar to a cell invaded by a virus.

This view faded at the end of the twentieth century, under the blows of numerous revisions that, even in today's pandemic situation, are very useful to understand the dialectic relationship between nucleic acids and proteins in the phenomenon of life. First of all, it has been found that DNA is always subjected to the action of epigenetic agents, causing methylation, or other protein molecules surrounding its structure, that influence the transcription process in to RNA, the molecule truly responsible for the protein synthesis that takes place at the cytoplasmic level. This shows that DNA is not at the helm of the phenotypic process, but is more like a recipe book that is consulted and whose recipes are sent to production or not depending on what the side elements allow to transcribe. There are two main consequences to this: i) there is no such thing as the linearity of the gene which imposes the protein translation, but rather there is an interaction between different components; ii) there is not only genetic inheritance, but also an epigenetic one (Di Mauro 2017), referring to those contouring factors which can silence, emphasize or identify a precise timing of genetic expression.

To this we should add that the "niche theory" (Hutchinson 1965; Odling-Smee 1988) has made this shift even stronger, because it sees organisms as the protagonists of their phylogenetic trajectory. In fact, through the action of modifying the environment, every living being transforms the matrix of selective pressures and, therefore, albeit indirectly, the morphopoiesis of the species. For some decades, several voices had risen to challenge the radically genocentric positions in morphopoiesis – I am thinking, for example, of the works of Patrick Bateson (2017) – so as to put the different forms of ontogenetic inheritance back at the center. It was known, for example, that in mammals the development of the individual is influenced by the environment, even if only through nutrition; but it is evident that any modification of the structure of the organism of the parent, under all aspects – for example, its endocrine setup or, more simply, the conformation of the pelvis – then affects the growth of the embryo. The reduction of an organ, moreover, never has a simple punctiform consequence, but alters the forces at work in morphopoiesis. We know, for example, that the contraction of the splanchnocranium in hominids has had repercussions in the remodeling of the head (Carrol 2006: 261–263), lowering the tension of the masseter muscles, followed by a progressive development of the neurocranium. However, the importance of the phenotype cannot be ignored because, in the final analysis, reproductive success depends on the performativity of the body: therein lies the litmus test of fitness.

But it is above all the mechanism of the organism's action on the environment that represents a turning point in marking the complexity of the evolutionary phenomenon. The body is never a passive entity in the environment, because it moves and colonizes new environments and above all because it is able to act by modifying the environment itself (Laland 2016: 191–202). This action exerts an indirect influence on morphopoiesis, since, by altering the environment, the individual acts on the selective factors, changing the pressures that reward one reproductive organism over another. Life on Earth cannot be compressed in an algorithm based on replicators, because Stephen J. Gould (1989) was right in stressing the importance of using the historical reading key in the events of phylogeny.

An animal population, in fact, is composed of subjects with different performative characteristics that cannot be reduced to the quantitative banality of the strongest or the best adapted. Every organism has fitness, that is, a reproductive advantage, on the basis of the conditions present in its operative field, so there is nothing that is better or worse in absolute terms. Rather, there is an individual who, in a given matrix of interconnected elements, that is, in the power relationship between selective factors, may or may not be advantaged. Now, we know that, as environmental characteristics change, something that sanctioned the success of one and the rejection of the other can be reversed: a camouflage coat color may become flashy or vice versa, a behavior that is useful for foraging may become unsuitable or even dangerous. We may believe that these interpretative transformations are simply the result of new discoveries, but in this case we would still be reasoning within the model of linearity: these discoveries are actually the result of a paradigm shift which, in turn, is the result of new discoveries, in a recursive relationship where it is difficult, useless and misleading to look for a *primum movens*. Certainly the thought of complexity (von Bertalanffy 1976; Ceruti 2018) has confronted us with new ways of considering the living, overcoming the classical mechanicism that was still prevailing in the twentieth, century.

On the other hand, the somatic dimension has powerfully emerged at the very moment when, for a curious paradox, the body found itself compressed not only in its social expression, but also in self-directed gestures, such as touching one's nose, carrying one's hands to one's mouth, rubbing one's eyes. The expression of the body is banned, wrapped in a robe of cautions and spontaneous manifestations that must be avoided. This, moreover, pushes us to look at the viral phenomenon no longer as a mere invasion of cells, but as a response of the organism itself to the infection. The body thus regains its centrality, moving away from an era which, in spite of countless scientific discoveries, had relegated it to a role of comprimario, denied even in its media overexposure.

4.3 In the Name of Animality

On the one hand, the revenge of the body highlights the limits of human ontological self-sufficiency, but on the other hand it seems to recall the dimension that we share with other species and that we call "animality." Hence the need to start again precisely from the presupposition that Jacques Derrida synthesized in *The Animal that Therefore I Am* (2008). Putting the body back at the center means revising the reading of the animal condition, no longer in terms of opposition, but as a flow of sharing between species. Tradition has given us an image of the nonhuman as totally passive, deprived of any form of protagonism: its expression has been described as a blind manifestation of genetic instructions or as the result of environmental conditioning. While every living being has both innate predispositions and learning processes, the error lies in the way these influences have been defined. Animal endowments have been interpreted as constraints rather than opportunities, real prisons that did not allow other species the same freedom and self-determination that human beings have.

Human and animal thus became opposite categories, in an ontological difference that found its full expression in Martin Heidegger (1992). The passivity of the animal, no longer heterospecific but categorically different from the human, was only the consequence of its instinctive and conditioned automatisms. The animal was therefore forced to play the part of a puppet moved by strings, in the logic of mechanistic passivity, which, from Jacques Loeb's (1916) chemical tropisms to Burrhus Skinner's (1938) behaviorism, explains behavior by resorting to its trigger. Instincts and conditionings recall viral entities which, from the past of phylogeny or from the stimulating action of the environment, invade and direct the animal. The nonhuman cannot have objectives, so its behavioral directionality is either governed by teleonomic algorithms (Monod 1970) or stimulated by a target: this means denying the animal any actual presence in the here and now. It cannot decide, judge, choose, program, simulate, design and cannot do so because this would contradict the model. The animal machine is therefore moved by switches which infect it – the impulses and stimuli – and, just like viruses, impose their functions.

Let us try, then, to question this model. First of all, we can say that there is no separation between innate and learned components, because every learning process uses the innate as starting material to shape new equipment, and likewise every predisposing innate structure needs learning to take a certain form. This means that the two factors, even within this dichotomy, are directly proportional to each other and therefore not complementary but dimensional: the more innate information there is, the greater the learning possibilities. The individuality of the animal is always a singular process which, as such, is unpredictable, and it is never possible to separate the phases of its realization. Ontogenesis is not an assembly of parts, but the construction of a system (Piaget 1997) – the integration into a whole that cannot be broken down.

Therefore, it is not a question of putting switches into the animal's body, but of building functional networks – we could imagine them as maps – that make more uses or routes available. The endowments are therefore tools and not automatisms: if on the one hand they influence the animal's behavior, on the other they are actively used by the animal (Marchesini 2013: 69–77). The difference between a tool and an automatism lies in the way we view the endowment itself: i) a tool lends itself to being used, because it has a range of possibilities of utilization and thanks to this gives ownership of use; ii) an automatism, on the contrary, is an imperative for the individual who can only undergo it. I would also like to underline that modeling the endowment as an instrument and not as an automatism leads us to a much more parsimonious explanatory formulation, that is, more respectful of Morgan's canon, since several functions can be carried out with the same instrument, but not with the same automatism.

But there is another reason why automatism is an incorrect model. Let's start from a very simple consideration: reality presents itself in a singular way to the individual, that is to say by predicates of *similarity* and not of identity, because the world presents itself to the subject every time with a margin of novelty, so the latter must be able to manage that novelty no matter how imperceptible it may be. In other words, for a living being it is not possible to simply repeat, that is, to let an automatism be triggered, in order to adhere to the opportunities of the world, but it must always make adjustments to the endowment or resort to it through innovative canons of use. This means that subjectivity is not an additional or high-level predicate of the living being – rather, it is the product of the very conformation of life.

Cognitive ethology, starting from the brilliant insights provided by Donald Griffin in *The Question of Animal Awareness* (1976), has highlighted how nonhuman species are also endowed with awareness, and this has undoubtedly represented a significant step forward in the understanding of animal behavior. Unfortunately, at the same time, he hinted that subjectivity is bound to intentionality, which inevitably lent itself to being evaluated according to the different gradients that each species presented, exposing itself to the very hierarchy that it was trying to avoid, placing the human being at the top of the cognitive pyramid of the living. In my opinion, it is a mistake to ground subjectivity in consciousness, for various reasons. The first concerns the fact that subjectivity must necessarily precede consciousness – as can be deduced from the very concept of the unconscious, but also from Benjamin Libet's elegant research (Libet 2004, 2012) – because subjectivity represents that inner world which consciousness enlightens, that is, makes explicit, but does not create. If intentionality is an expression of referentiality (Brentano 1874–1911) – a "being aware" of something – that something must precede the process of making it explicit. Therefore, it is necessary to revise the concept of subjectivity, in order to be able to account for the "being a bearer of inherent interests" – that is, self-ownership – which manifests itself in expressive protagonism.

Moreover, before ascending to the higher levels of animal cognition, it is necessary to modify the explanatory paradigm of the basic condition of animality – that is, the model we adopt to say what an animal is, that is, what its metapredicates are – by overcoming the mechanistic explanation that denies the nonhuman a real presence in the here and now. This is why I suggested the importance of abandoning the descriptive reflection typical of scientific ethology, only interested in explaining the predicates, that is, how the animal machine works. What is needed instead is a reflection on the model itself, which goes beyond the mechanistic vision of the animal – that is, a reflection grounded in philosophical ethology (Bussolini, Buchanan & Chrulew 2018: 21–45). Indeed, it would be useless to attribute consciousness to an entity without protagonism, that is, indifferent to what is happening and not projected towards the world: this kind of entity could never give rise to a subjectivity which, on the contrary, manifests itself in being interested in the possibilities offered by the world.

The mechanic interpretation of the animal adheres to the *res extensa* model that foresees the intervention of an external factor to justify its presence in the world; in this sense this explanation of behavior must appeal to a principle that recalls the infection. Only by overcoming dualism is it possible, on the contrary, to give protagonism back to the animal condition, acknowledging that all organisms are "bearers of interests", a condition which underpins their active participation in the world. Subjectivity is mainly expressed in emotional feelings and motivational desires, that is, intrinsic qualities that in their load of interests represent copulae towards the external reality and therefore motors of experiential singularity: this is the condition of dialogical being, by which the animal is not closed in itself but exists in a continuous constructive relationship with the world (Shaeffer 2007).

In my opinion, there are five presuppositions that allow us to clarify the metapredicative condition of animality: i) the principle of relationality, for which being an animal means constructing multiple planes of diachronic relationship, for example, by bringing back to the subject the events of the past and building a relationship with the world that is always in progress; ii) the principle of creativity, for which an animal never limits itself to repeating but is always the owner of the endowment it possesses, so it cannot but be creative in the actions it carries out, because it must always invent its present; iii) the desiring principle, which makes animals always proactive and capable of transforming the world into a field of action, being endowed with internal motivations that lead them to act and to transform phenomena into epiphanies, that is, into events to be brought back to themselves, constructing problems that they then try to solve; 4) the principle of sentience, given by the emotional character that ensures that external events are always reported, that is, endowed with value for themselves and therefore somatized, so that the sensible body of an animal is not limited to the perimeter of its skin but extends to the events that affect it; 5) the emergence principle, for which there is no one place for subjectivity, as it cannot concern a single part of the body or a particular function, and it cannot be assigned to a *res cogitans*, a *homunculus* or consciousness, because subjectivity is a function spread throughout the matrix of physiological experience.

We often affirm that the differences between human beings and other species are simply quantitative, but even this is a mistake, because it does not question evaluative anthropocentrism, as if humans could really stand as a measurement unit for the other species. Such a vision starts from the assumption that human beings do not have biological specializations, that is, they are a larval and indefinite entity which, as such, is neutral as well as free, because it is not confined in any ecological niche. Even Darwinism was therefore forced within the humanistic framework, interpreting human evolution not as a process of specialization, as could also be found in other animals, but as an event of human emancipation from the animal condition. The banalization of Charles Darwin's thought in the statement "human beings derive from animals" suggests that they now belong to a different dimension, pushing any animal remains back into a remote past of which only a few traces remain, submerged in the depths of instinct and the unconscious. This interpretation of animality has transformed the other species into a sort of "dark mirror" from which to take leave in order to recover the fullness of the human condition, something to be avoided in its feral drifts as an infection that calls for resolute prophylactic action.

At most we now say that we have an animal part (the animal that is in me), but not that we *are* an animal (the animal that I am), so that the human condition is not seen as a declination of animality but as emancipation from it. In my opinion this paradigm does not allow us to truly understand the human condition and to come to terms with what we are (Merleau-Ponty 2013). The big problem, however, is that should we claim to be nothing more than one of the many expressions of animality, we would still fall back into the image of the animal condition formulated by Western tradition, which inevitably brings us back into the game of dichotomies. If I say that humans are animals, I am not saying that they correspond to that disfigured image of the animal that humanism has left us. If we want to understand the human animal, that is to say the human being as a declination of animality, we must necessarily emancipate animality first, that is, we must reject its role of antithesis. Otherwise we will always fall back into the traditional dichotomy.

By emptying animality of its contents, anthropocentrism has undoubtedly contributed to seeing the body as nothing more than a container and, more generally, to viewing nature as nothing more than a set of resources to be infected for the sole self-centered purpose of human affirmation on the world. We might think that a reflection on animality is not relevant to understand the critical issues we are experiencing, assuming that it can all be remedied simply through the etiquette of eco-sustainable behavior, but this, in my opinion, is exactly the greatest danger we face today. We must have the strength to admit that the problems we are facing are the result of anthropocentrism, in all its forms and not only those concerning ethics, because it represents the biggest obstacle to understanding the disjunction that has been created between us and the living world. We cannot continue to attribute the innumerable emergencies to simple accidents. It is essential to sew up the network that has been torn apart under the weight of the anthropocentric assumption – a view that today is clearly showing all its fallacies. Anthropocentrism is the real enemy of the human being. So, I would like to reformulate Terence's famous sentence in these terms: *Animal sum, animalis nihil a me alienum.*

5 The Posthumanist View

5.1 Premise

The pandemic brought to the surface some weaknesses in the prevailing social and development model that had remained somewhat in the shadows, in the presumption that, after all, our habits would continue as always, under the reassuring umbrella of stability and invisible hands capable of self-regulation (Smith, 1776).

We cannot understand the deep-seated reasons for the emergencies that humanity is experiencing by remaining on the surface of the problem, as if it all amounted simply to a misguided use of environmental resources. The current emergency is the result of a cultural paradigm based on the disconnection of the human being from nature, an ontological presupposition that has severed all belonging, sharing and contamination with the nonhuman and that we can define in a single word: anthropocentrism. This term is undoubtedly abused and can be interpreted in very different ways – however, it is often regarded as the inevitable condition of the human being. For this reason I want to clarify what I mean. Anthropocentrism is not about the perspective with which we inevitably observe and interpret phenomena, nor is it about our natural pursuit of the interest of our species. It is a very precise cultural assumption that has become established in Western philosophy, feeding on different contributions but converging in a precise consideration of the relationship between us and the community of the living (Plato, *Protagoras*; Augustine of Hippo, *De Civitate Dei contra Paganos*). The anthropocentric assumption, in fact, traces a clear disjunction between the human being and everything else, placing our species above nature, so that no dependencies, sharing or hybridizations are allowed.

The entire biosphere, considered external and in some ways alien to the human condition, has taken on the role of a living dimension (environment), a backdrop or stage to highlight the special character of the human race (antithesis), a source of goods to be consumed (resource) or a continent to be explored to increase our knowledge, which in turn can be translated into technological applications useful for the progress and affirmation of *Homo sapiens*.

Not even a virus can claim to be free from ecological balances (O'Malley 2016: 71–79). The claim to release identity from relationship clashes with the logic of the living and with the very character of the human, which is as interrelated as it could be. Not only are we linked to other living beings by ecological and epidemiological interdependencies and by sharing precepts and conditions, but it is our own cultural dimension that bears witness to the hybrid nature of the human condition. Culture, in fact, represents the best example of the relational nature of the human being, since all cultural expressions – dance, music, technology, fashion, to give a few examples – are the result of hybridization processes of our species with other living beings (Marchesini 2017: 71–91)

When Peter Sloterdijk, in his anthropotechnical account *You Must Change Your Life* (2014), imagines a continuous verticalization of the individual through the exercise of immunity, he outlines a tightrope walker who must constantly train to keep a distance from the ground. This sense of estrangement of the human being from nature, which runs throughout Western thought and propagates our acrobatics of distinction, can be considered the beating heart of anthropocentrism. As long as we experience this non-belonging despite inhabiting this planet, and as long as we represent ourselves as nomadic and volatile entities with respect to the biosphere, freed from the network of interdependencies, we will not be able to get out of this destructive dead end, because every action of ours, no matter how harmful, will always find good reasons to be taken. If, instead, we are able to understand that the human condition itself is the result of an infection contracted with the world, that there is no purity in human predicates, that what we value most in our species – those cultural connotations we so boast of – are the fruit of the copulatory character of our nature and the precious contribution of otherness, then we will be finally able to take a different path and make different choices as a consequence.

Thus, to rediscover the meaning of relationship is the imperative of our time, re-reading Sloterdijk's trajectory no longer as an ascension, but as a horizontal widening over the world, going back to what Donna Haraway called "sympoiesis" (2016) and I have defined as "heteronomy", that is, openness of all qualities to the contribution of the other (Marchesini 2018a: 98).

5.2 Anthropocentrisms

In order to question the anthropocentric structure, it is necessary first of all to clarify what is meant by this term-concept, which in its etymological meaning simply indicates the act of placing the *anthropos* at the center, without stating which aspect of this notion is referred to and possibly rejected. I would like to address, in particular, two tendencies: i) considering the human being in terms of a neutral and universal perspective, credited as a measure of the world; ii) considering the human condition as an autonomous and self-founded construction, interpreting cultural constructions as solipsistic expressions of human ingenuity.

But in order to understand what is meant by anthropocentrism, which is to all intents and purposes a cultural construction and not a biological fact, it is essential first of all to differentiate it from the "anthropocentric perspective", that is to say from that particular point of view that makes the human being refer to the world through the logic of self-reference and partiality. This perspective evolved during the phylogenetic process which, having fashioned particular sensory organs, has developed in our species an interpretative perspective of the phenomena. This was described in an exemplary way by Konrad Lorenz in *Behind The Mirror* (1978), where the Kantian a priori are explained as evolutionary a posteriori, that is, as experiences acquired by our ancestors and therefore able to speak about the world. Can we, then, move away from or at least suspend the anthropocentric perspective? Surely we cannot totally withdraw from it or abandon it because, being human, we must necessarily appeal to our connotations in order to be able to access reality. On the other hand, the anthropocentric perspective, which can also be defined as "naive physics" (Bozzi 1999) or "intuitionism", is the starting point, but is subject to continuous redefinition. The tendency of human beings to identify with others, a quality that can be ascribed to their deeply empathic and mimetic nature, has allowed us to widen our gaze beyond the anthropocentric visual angle. Instruments and machines have also led to perspective shifts and scientific experience itself can be considered as a process of prospective anthropo-decentralization (Bachelard 1934).

If the anthropocentric perspective is nothing more than the species-specific way of approaching the world, epistemological anthropocentrism is the negation of such partiality, in the presumption that the human being is a neutral entity that, therefore, can stand as a unit of measurement of the world. This assumption is well represented by Leonardo da Vinci's *Vitruvian Man*, a work that has become the image-manifesto of a centrality that not only rises above the depths of nature, but also sets itself as a measure of the world. This brings me to the second level of anthropocentrism, the ontological one, which considers the human being certainly not as an animal, but as the nonanimal by definition, an entity that is not embedded within a niche and is therefore free and autopoietic, because it lacks adaptive specializations. According to this form of anthropocentrism, human beings are different from an essential point of view, so that they cannot be compared to a particular species, but to the animal category as a whole.

They are special, not specific, because they are capable of self-determination, unlike animals that are presumed to be unable to build their own destiny. In this view, not only is there a constitutive or genealogical ontological difference, but it is also believed that every aspect of the human condition and cultural dimension – what some authors call "anthropo-poiesis" (Guerci 2007) – is an autarkic construction, that is, the exclusive product of our ingenuity. In this emanatory reading of the predicates, it is believed that human beings can be understood *according to their own principles*, that is, through an internal reconnaissance and without taking into account the relationships contracted with the nonhuman universe.

On the other hand, questioning ontological anthropocentrism does not only concern the revision of the specialty status based on the theory of incompleteness, but also and above all the idea that the human condition, in its aspects of cultural dimensioning, is the result of an autarkic process: that is, of solipsistic operations of human ingenuity or of compensation for our presumed adaptive shortcomings. The human condition is the most hybrid condition that can be found in nature and this is precisely because of some phylogenetic characteristics of our species, such

as: i) the great development of our brain and especially of the prefrontal associa-
tive areas; ii) the neonatal immaturity and the long duration of our development;
iii) the strong imitative motivation, which has transformed every phenomenon
into an epiphany; iv) the parental care towards juvenile forms, which has allowed
for the mothering of the young of other species and the development of multi-
species communities; v) the propensity for collecting, cataloguing and collecting,
which has transformed biodiversity into the first orientation guideline; vi) the
tendency towards exploration and nomadism, which has widened the living
environment of the human being; vii) the anatomical characteristics, which
have facilitated the manufacture and use of tools, making the body increasingly
adherent to external means; viii) the high level of competitiveness of our species.

These characteristics are to be considered as flywheels of *hybridization with*
the world, not as the qualities which have favored *isolation from* the world. The
human being has always been an entity in becoming, the humanistic reading is
right about that, but such becoming should not be read in the vertical directionality of ascension and emancipation from nature, but in the horizontal one of
progressive contamination with otherness. If we can understand this being-at-
one with the world, our debt to the nonhuman and our strong connection to the
world from an ontological point of view, we will not only be able to recognize
the importance of relationship, but we will have the opportunity to better
understand the roots of our own condition.

5.3 Dialogo Ergo Sum

Moving from a disjunctive to a relational vision means, becoming aware of
interdependence – not only ecological, biological, epidemiological, but above
all ontological. This means first of all admitting the existential principle, inherent
in relationship, that makes every quality come about by emergence, that is, in the
encounter between entities and in the supervening of their qualities. I am unable
here to delve into this hybridative disposition of human beings, which leads them
to wear skins to assume the virtues of another species, to welcome wolves into
their community and thus reinvent their hunting strategies, to transform the
courting rituals of birds into propitiatory dances and so on (Armstrong 1942:
182–205). But the human dimension lies precisely in this dream.

Talking about a relational ontology or eco-ontology, therefore, means overcoming the essentialist reading and understanding that the human being lies in
relationship, not in disjunction. It means recognizing that the humanist claim of
total emancipation of the human being from nature has betrayed the copulatory
principle that lies at the root of anthropo-poiesis itself. To affirm a relational
ontology means, therefore, neither to fall into antihumanism nor to reject the

great innovations of early humanism, but to avoid the anthropocentric drift of modernity and thus carry forward the revolutionary principles of rediscovery of the body and the hybrid character of the somatic dimension of early humanism. In this sense it is correct to speak of "posthumanism", a departure from the great intuitions of the fifteenth century which does not betray the valorization of human predicates, but assigns them to an eco-ontological dimension. We could say, then, that posthumanist philosophy calls into question the disjunctive and essentialist principles, namely the views according to which: i) the human being is opposed to animality, considered instead as nothing more than one of the possible expressions of animality; ii) the human condition is realized through autopoiesis, believing on the contrary that it emerges in the exchange with otherness; iii) the outcome of the cultural dimensioning gives rise to a disjunction and a verticalization, thinking vice versa that it increases the conjunction with other living forms and lies in horizontality.

The post-humanist proposal, therefore, especially in the guise that has characterized the Italian philosophical approach (Ferrando 2019; Iovino, Marchesini, & Adorni 2016; Braidotti 2019), starts precisely from questioning such a distancing interpretation, by proposing, instead of the image of verticalization or ascension of the human from the telluric, a hybrid conception or a close relationship with otherness for the construction of the human predicates themselves. For this reason, the posthuman, as a key figure of reference, is not given by a species-specific horizon of the human being, but by the advent of a nascent awareness of existential interdependence. Hence a real ontological conversion, capable of rediscovering the human being as relationship and as participation, proposing, instead of the humanist figure of the tightrope walker, that of a diver who plunges into the deep. If human predicates are conceived as outcomes of the relationship with the nonhuman, it becomes evident that everything we recognize as characterizing our condition is the result of decentralization. The human dimension, in its predicates, does not derive from withdrawing from the world, but from decentralizing from the anthropocentric closure, recognizing oneself within a continuous flow of loans. This paradigm shift shows how illusory it is to claim some human alleged purity and distance from any form of contamination – which, moreover, has been the source of many aberrations and evils (Douglas, 2002) – grounding human nature in separation and self-reference.

5.4 Infectious Dynamics

The pandemic has surprised and frightened us, and it has certainly slowed down the world economy and suspended established habits; perhaps it has even made us reflect on the sustainability of a certain development model, even if it is easy for us to eventually resume our habits as if we had learned nothing. However, the still-open wound of what happened and the discovery of being so vulnerable have led to a generalized feeling of prophylactic demand which, if understandable now, must be overcome. We cannot, in fact, imagine ourselves in a germ-free dimension, because every organism is an ecosystem and life is always a laboratory of relationships, and viruses play an important part in this network. We have the impression that a virus is something objectively negative, against which we must defend ourselves, and yet this view is not only incorrect, but risks inspiring policies of everyday medication and control of socio-ecological relations that would have the opposite effect (Illich 1982). In reality, our metabolism bases its functions on the joint action of symbionts that inhabit our body in various ways, and the immune system itself is strengthened through interaction with the vast universe of antigens it encounters, so we need this coexistence.

But if that is the case, what are the causes of such a devastating contagion? It's not easy to answer. I would be tempted to dismiss the argument by saying that perhaps it is we who are wrong to persist in believing that the order of nature is based on harmony and stability, because, on the contrary, catastrophes are an integral part of life on Earth and even our very existence can be erased at any time. This is certainly true, but it is a partial response. While it is true that there is dynamism in *bios* and that sometimes catastrophic passages occur, nevertheless biological logics tend to build homeostasis, able to buffer perturbations and gradually adapt to changes. They succeed in this anchoring process through multiple relationships, which take place over very long evolutionary times, so that what at the beginning presents itself as a selective pressure on the single organism – we could say, an enemy – with the unfolding of generations becomes the chiseler of the qualities of that species and likewise the site of symbiotic interactions that ensure homeostatic stability.

When, however, we expose ourselves to relationships for which we are not equipped from a phylogenetic point of view, we inevitably start coevolutionary processes that have a disastrous impact in the short term. The lesson we should learn, therefore, is the importance of acting with caution on ecosystems, because what in one circumstance can be a factor of stability, in another can take on the role of a catastrophic flywheel. Viruses have played a fundamental role in phylogeny (Margulis 1999) and are central entities in the stabilization of ecosystems and therefore in the maintenance of the species, so infection is part of the logic of the living – it is no accident. But, just as carbon dioxide represents the basic material for the constitution of vital energy, thanks to photosynthetic action, so a threshold upheaval of this element could represent the end of life on our planet. Therefore, the lesson we must learn is not specifically about Covid-19, but about the very meaning of relational ontology.

The virus and, more generally, the logic of the infection may seem like a metaphor, but from my point of view they are more of a reading key, a real paradigm which aims to explain biological relations and therefore also our own dimension, which only from an anthropocentric point of view we continue to think of as transcendent. If, on the other hand, we learn to understand the relational basis from which our individuality emerges – that is, the fact that we are not an essence that qualifies itself through purity and disjunction, but rather an interweaving of relationships, from the interaction of which emergent qualities develop – then we will finally be able to look at the world with new eyes, attentive to connecting structures rather than introspection. And if, likewise, we keep in mind that such relationships can be the homeostatic foundation as well as the greatest disruptive factor, then we will understand that it is necessary to stabilize the thresholds instead of building phantom walls. Hospitable relationships, set up through gradual and progressive processes of integration, are what ensure the strength of an entity, not the act of clinging to a supposed purity of identity: this makes it clear that the logic of infection supports every expression of life.

Viruses must be considered as specific biological entities, so it is inappropriate to speak of computer viruses or memes as cultural viruses. Likewise, it is wrong to think that every entity, simply because it gives rise to infectious and hybrid processes, acts like a virus. However, the logic of the virus can show us in an extremely clear and, if you like, counterintuitive way, the infectiously relational nature of the living being, precisely because it relies on external metabolic structures and influences their physiology. A virus cannot exist outside of a relational condition: it cannot do so because, explicitly, in order to reproduce it needs to use a xenobiotic apparatus. But, if we think about it, no living being can exist outside an articulated number of relationships and external dependencies, so life itself is sustained and regulated by external entities. These relations are what produce those qualities that, due to an error of perspective, we attribute in an essentialistic way to the entity itself.

The virus, therefore, can be used as a model to understand this paradigm shift that we have before us and which can no longer be postponed, if we want to give a future to our presence on the world's stage. We use nouns such as contagion, contamination, infection, and adjectives such as spurious, dirty, impure to depict something negative to avoid, as opposed to what is immaculate, authentic, aseptic, which corresponds to that ideal of purity, essence, identity, coherence that still pervades our programs. And yet the ecological dimension is anything but! Life is continuous contamination, it is construction of structures through syncytial and symbiotic practices; it is affirmation of complex organisms whose cells, for a considerable percentage, do not belong to the genome of a given species. In nature, organisms are anything but pure and they function thanks to complex mutualisms or infections that construct articulated synergies over time. On the contrary, sterile and pure is what corresponds to death – it is the coldness of crystal, not the sticky permeability and infiltrativeness of life. It is necessary, then, to assume full awareness that it is not possible to find assonance with the biosphere while remaining attached to a paradigm that denies the elementary logic of life.

I cannot say whether we will be able to fully understand how far our thinking has strayed from sharing and belonging to the community of the living, whether we will realize that our destructive actions are not just reckless gestures, but represent the coherent consequences of a certain way of conceiving the human. I believe that the pandemic has undoubtedly shaken us, but the human being is also inclined to forget, and the current wake-up call could very well sound remote soon. However, the dimension of contagion may perhaps go beyond its epidemiological perimeter and assume a paradigmatic dimension, providing us with new models for interpreting our presence in the world. It is understandable that, in the face of an emergency of epochal proportions, defensive reactions will prevail and instruct the immediate strategies of containment, but it is indispensable, later on, to look beyond the contingency. We are a virus for the planet, but at the same time we are subject to continuous infections, and it is those infections that have designed the undoubted masterpiece that we call the human condition. Having greater awareness of our hybrid dimension can help us to rediscover the value of being in a relationship and to understand that the extension of the human is not limited to the contours of our skin.

Bibliography

Adams, Carol (2015). *The Sexual Politics of Meat*. London: Bloomsbury Academic.

Afifi, Tamer et al. (2018). "Wired: The Impact of Media and Technology Use on Stress (Cortisol) and Inflammation (interleukin Il- 6) in Fast Paced Families". *Computers in Human Behaviour*, 81: 265–273.

Agamben, Giorgio (2020). "Sul vero e sul falso". Online column by Giorgio Agamben. *Quodlibet*. https://www.quodlibet.it/giorgio-agamben-sul-vero-e-sul-falso.

Alfano Miglietti, Francesca (2008). *Identità mutanti, dalla piega alla piaga*. Milano: Bruno Mondadori.

Andreoli, Bruno & Montanari, Massimo (1995). *Il bosco nel Medioevo*, Bologna: Clueb.

Applebaum, Anne (2020). "Le epidemie favoriscono i governi autoritari". *Internazionale*, 4. https://www.internazionale.it/opinione/anne-applebaum/2020/03/28/epidemie-governi-autoritari?.

Armstrong, Edward A. (1942). *Bird Display and Behaviour. An Introduction to the Study of Bird Psychology*. Cambridge: Cambridge University Press.

Augé, Marc (1999). *Disneyland e altri nonluoghi*. Torino: Bollati Boringhieri.

Bachelard, Gaston (1934). *Le nouvel esprit scientifique*. Paris: Les Presses Universitaires de France.

Bateson, Patrick (2017). *Behaviour, Development and Evolution*. Cambridge: Open Book Publishers.

Bauerfeind, Rolf, et al. (2016). *Zoonoses, Infectious Disease Transmissible from Animals to Human*. Washington, DC: American Society for Microbiology.

Bauman, Zygmunt (2000). *Liquid Modernity*. Cambridge: Polity Press.

Ben-Barak, Idan (2008). *Small Wonders. How Microbes Rule Our World*. Carlton North, Australia: Scribe Publication.

Bethke, Bruce (1980). "Cyberpunk", *Amazing Science Fiction Stories, 57*, 4.

Bonneuil, Christophe & Fressoz, Jean-Baptiste (2013). *L'événement Anthropocène: La terre, l'histoire et nous*. Paris: Editions du Seuil.

Bostrom, Nick (2014). *Superintelligence. Paths, Dangers, Strategies*. Oxford: Oxford University Press.

Bozzi, Paolo (1999). *Fisica ingenua. Studi di Psicologia della Percezione*. Milano: Garzanti.

Bradbury, Ray (2013). *Fahrenheit 451*. London: HarperCollins.

Braidotti, Rosi (2019). *Posthuman Knowledge*. Cambridge: Polity.

Brainard, George, Hanifin, John, Greeson, Jeffrey et al. (2001). "Action Spectrum for Melatonin Regulation in Humans: Evidence for a Novel Circadian Photoreceptor". *The Journal Of Neuroscience*, 21, 16: 6405–6412.

Brentano, Franz (1874–1911). *Psychologie vom empirischen Standpunkt*, Hamburg: Felix Meiner Verlag.

Brooks, Samantha K., Webster, Rebecca K. , Smith, Louise E. , et al. (2020). "The Psychological Impact of Quarantine and How to Reduce It: Rapid Review of the Evidence". *Lancet*, 395: 912–920.

Buffetaut, Eric (1993). *Grandi estinzioni e crisi biologiche*. Milano: Jaca Book.

Bussolini, Jeffrey, Buchanan, Brett & Chrulew, Matthew (2018). *The Philosophical Ethology of Roberto Marchesini*, London: Routledge.

Butler, Judith (2016). *Precarious Life*. London: Verso Books.

Butler, Judith (2020b). *The Force of Non-violence*. London: Verso Books.

Butler, Judith (30 March 2020a). "Capitalism Has its Limits". *Verso Blog*. https://www.versobooks.com/blogs/4603-capitalism-has-its-limits

Byung-Chul, Han (2015). *The Burnout Society*, Stanford: Stanford University Press.

Caffo, Leonardo (2020). *Dopo il Covid-19, punti per una discussione*. Roma: Nottetempo.

Campbell, Neil A., Reece, Jane B. & Simon, Eric J. (2007). *Essential Biology*. Harlow: Pearson.

Carroll, Sean B. (2006). *Endless Forms Most Beautiful*. London: Weidenfeld & Nicolson.

Carson, Rachel (1962). *Silent Spring*. Boston: Houghton Mifflin.

Cassandro, Daniele (2020). "Siamo in guerra! Il coronavirus e le sue metafore", *Internazionale*, 3. https://www.internazionale.it/opinione/daniele-cassandro/2020/03/22/coronavirus-metafore-guerra.

Ceruti, Mauro (2018). *Il tempo della complessità*, Milano: Raffaello Cortina.

Cignini, Bruno (2019). *Animali in città*. Roma: Lapis Edizioni.

Ciuffoletti, Zeffiro (1993). *Retorica del complotto*. Milano: Il Saggiatore.

Crick, Francis (1970). "Central Dogma of Molecular Biology". *Nature*, 227: 561–563.

Dawkins, Richard (1976). *The Selfish Gene*. Oxford: Oxford University Press.

de Kerckhove, Derrick (1991). *Brainframes: Technology, Mind and Business*. Utrecht: Bosch & Keuning.

Dehaene, Stanislas (2019). *How We Learn, Why Brain Learn Better than Any Machine*. New York: Viking.

Deleuze, Gilles & Guattari, Felix (1978–1980). "Bodies Without Organs". In *Anti-Oedipus: Capitalism and Schizophrenia*. Minneapolis: University of Minnesota Press.

Demichelis, Lelio (2018). *La grande alienazione: Narciso, Pigmalione, Prometeo e il tecno-capitalismo*. Milano: Jaca book.

Dennett, Daniel (2003). *Freedom Evolves*. New York: Viking Press.

Dennett, Daniel (2004). *Darwin's Dangerous Idea: Evolution and the Meaning of Life*. New York: Simon & Schuster.

Derrida, Jacques (2008). *The Animal That Therefore I Am*. New York: Fordham University Press.

Di Mauro, Ernesto (2017). *Epigenetica il DNA che impara. Istruzioni per l'uso del patrimonio genetico*. Trieste: Asterios.

Diamond, Jared (1997). *Guns, Germs and Steel: The Fates of Human Societies*. New York: W.W. Norton & Company.

Doucleff, Michaeleen (2018). *Are there zombie viruses in the thawing permafrost*. NPR, 1. https://www.npr.org/sections/goatsandsoda/2018/01/24/575974220/are-there-zombie-viruses-in-the-thawing-permafrost#

Douglas, Mary (2002). *Purity and Danger*. London: Routledge.

Doyle R. (1996). *Wetwares: Experiments in Postvital Living*. London: ShoreBooks.

Dozois, Gardner (1984). "Science Fiction in the Eighties", *Washington Post*. December 30.

Drexler, Eric (1986). *Engines of Creation*. New York: Doubleday.

Drlica, Karl & Perlin, David S. (2011). *Antibiotic Resistance, Understanding and Responding to an Emerging Crisis*. Upper Saddle River: Pearson Education Inc.

Eco, Umberto (2016). *Il superuomo di massa. Retorica ed ideologia del romanzo popolare*. Milano: La nave di Teseo.

Ehrlich, Paul R. (1995). *The Population Bomb*. New York: Buccaneer Books.

Ellis, Erle C. (2018). *Anthropocene: A Very Short Introduction*. New York: Oxford University Press.

Emerson, Ralph W. (1836). *Nature*. Boston: James Munroe and Company.

Esposito, Roberto (2011). *Immunitas: The Protection and Negation of Life*. Cambridge: Polity Press.

Ferrando, Francesca (2019). *Philosophical Posthumanism*. New York: Bloomsbury Academic.

Foucault, Michel (1961). *Folie et déraison. Histoire de la folie à l'age classique*. Paris: Plon.

Fry, Iris (2000). *The Emergence of Life on Earth*. New Brunswick: Rutgers University Press.

Gehlen, Arnold (1940). *Der Mensch. Seine Natur und seine Stellung in der Welt.* (Translated Mcmillan, Clare and Pillmer, Karl (1987). *Man: His Nature and Place in the World.* New York: Columbia University Press).

Gibson, William (1982). "Burning Chrome", *Omni*, July.

Gould, Stephen J. (1989). *Wonderful Life: The Burgess Shale and the Nature of History.* New York: Norton & Company.

Gould, Stephen J. (1991). *Bully for Brontosaurus, Reflections in Natural History.* New York: W.W. Norton & Company.

Gourhan, André Leroi (1945). *L'Homme et la matière.* Paris: Éditions Albin Michel.

Grant, Sara & Olsen, Christopher W. (1999). "Preventing Zoonotic Diseases in Immunocompromised Person: The Role of Physicians and Veterinarians". *Emerging Infectious Diseases*, 5: 159–163.

Greenfield, Susan (2015). *Mind Change – How Digital Technology Is Living Their Mark On Our Brains.* New York: Random House.

Griffin, Donald (1976). *The Question of Animal Awareness.* New York: The Rockefeller University Press.

Guerci, Antonio (2007). *Dall'antropologia all'antropopoiesi: breve saggio sulle rappresentazioni e costruzioni della variabilità umana.* Milano: Cristina Lucisano Editore.

Guppy, Daryl (2020). "The Wet Markets and Western Myths". *CGTN.* https://news.cgtn.com/news/2020-04-11/The-wet-markets-and-the-western-myths-PBJKbseZ9K/index.html

Hamerschlag, Kari and EWG Senior Analyst (2011). Environmental Working Group. What You Eat Matters. www.ewg.org/meateatersguide.

Haraway, Donna J. (2016). *Staying with the Trouble, Making Kin in Chthulucene.* Durham: Duke University Press.

Hardin, Garrett (1974). "Lifeboat Ethics: the Case against Helping the Poor". *Psychology Today*, 8, 38–43

Haughton, Ciaran, Aiken, Mary & Cheevers, Carly (2015). "Cyber Babies: the Impact of Emerging Technology on the Developing Infant". *Psychology Research*, 5: 504–518.

Heidegger, Martin (1992). *The Fundamental Concepts of Metaphysics, World, Finitude, Solitude.* Bloomington: Indiana University Press.

Higuchi, Susumu et al. (2014). "Influence of Light at Night on Melatonin Suppression in Children". *The Journal of Clinical Endocrinology & Metabolism*, 99, 9: 3298–3303.

Houghton, John (2015). *Global Warming, The Complete Briefing.* Cambridge: Cambridge University Press.

Hurst, Christon J. (2000). *Viral Ecology.* Cambridge: Academic Press.

Hutchinson, George E. (1965). *The Ecological Theatre and the Evolutionary Play*. New Haven: Yale University Press.

Ikemoto, Satoshi & Panksepp, Jaak. (1999), "The Role Of Nucleus Accumbens Dopamine In Motivated Behavior: A Unifying Interpretation With Special Reference To Rewards Seeking". *Brain Research BR Reviews*, 31: 6–41.

Illich, Ivan (1982). *Medical Nemesis: The Expropriation of Health*, New York: Pantheon.

Imeson, Anton (2012). *Desertification, Land Degradation and Sustainability*. Hoboken: Wiley-Blackwell.

Iovino, Serenella, Marchesini, Roberto & Adorni, Eleonora (2016). "Past the Human: Narrative, Ontologies and Ontological Stories". *Relations*, 4.1.

IPCC Report (2019). *Global Warming of 1.5°*. Intergovernmental Panel on Climate Change. https://www.ipcc.ch/site/assets/uploads/sites/2/2019/06/SR15_Full_Report_High_Res.pdf

Ismail, Ramsey (2018). *Not Working, Working from Home: The Work of Hikikomori*. San Diego: University of California.

Jacobs, Karen & Baker, Nancy A. (2002). "The Association Between Children's Computer Use And Musculoskeletal Discomfort". *Work*, 18: 221–226.

Jonas, Hans (1984). *The Imperative of Responsibility: In Search of an Ethics for the Technological Age*, Chicago: University of Chicago Press.

Jones-Dion's, Nicole (2017). *Stasis*, United States.

Kimsa, Magdalena C. et al. (2014). "Porcine Endogenous Retroviruses in Xenotransplantation-Molecular Aspects". *Viruses*, 6: 2062–2083.

Kolbert, Elizabeth (2014). *The Sixth Extinction, an Unnatural History*. New York: Henry Holt & C.

Kon, Kateryna & Rai, Mahendra (2016). *Antibiotic Resistance, Mechanism and New Antimicrobial Approaches*. San Diego: Elsevier.

Laland, Kevin, Blake, Matthews & Feldman, Marcus W. (2016). "An Introduction to Niche Construction Theory". *Evolutionary Ecology*, 30: 191–202.

Lanternari, Vittorio (2003). *Ecoantropologia, dall'ingerenza ecologica alla svolta etico culturale*. Bari: Dedalo.

Làzlò, Ervin (2006). *The Chaos Point: The World at the Crossroads*. New York: Hampton Press.

Le Moli, Andrea (2020). "Pandemia e vita animale". *Il rasoio di Occam. Micromega*, 4. http://ilrasoiodioccam-micromega.blogautore.espresso.repubblica.it/2020/04/03/pandemia-e-vita-animale

Levantesi, Stella (9 April 2020). "L'epidemiologo Snowden: 'Questa pandemia specchio di una globalizzazione letale'". *Il Manifesto*. https://ilmanifesto.it/

lepidemiologo-snowden-la-pandemia-specchio-di-una-globalizzazione-letale-serve-lassistenza-sanitaria-universale/

Lewis, Simon L. & Maslin, Mark A. (2018). *Human Planet, How We Created the Anthropocene.* London: Pelican Book.

Libet, Benjamin (2004). *Mind Time. The Temporal Factor in Consciousness.* Cambridge: Harvard University Press.

Libet, Benjamin (2012). *Neurophysiology of Consciousness.* Basel: Birkhäuser.

Loeb, Jacques (1916). *The Organism as a Whole: From a Physicochemical Viewpoint.* New York: G.P. Putnam's Sons.

Lorenz, Konrad (1978). *Behind The Mirror: A Search for a Natural History of Human Knowledge.* Boston: Houghton Mifflin.

Lovelock, James E. (1979). *Gaia. A New Look at Life on Earth.* Oxford: Oxford Landmark Science.

Luca, Fabiana, "Borrell all'Europarlamento: 'Nel mondo post-coronavirus rischi di populismo e derive autoritarie'". *Eunews*, 4. https://www.eunews .it/2020/04/20/borrell-europarlamento-nel-mondo-post-coronavirus-rischi-populismo-derive-autoritarie/129206

Lundin, Susanne (2015). *Organs for Sale.* London: Palgrave McMillian.

Mainardi, Danilo (2016). *La città degli animali.* Milano: Cairo Editore.

Mallapaty, Smriti (2020). "Animal source of the coronavirus continues to elude scientists". *Nature.* https://www.nature.com/articles/d41586-020-01449-8

Malmstrom, Carolyn M. (2018). *Advances in Virus Research, Environmental Virology and Virus Ecology.* Cambridge: Academic Press.

Manca, Maura & Petrone, Loredana (2014). *La rete e il bullismo, il bullismo nella rete*, Roma: Alpes Italia.

Marchesini, Roberto (1996). *Il concetto di soglia.* Roma: Theoria.

Marchesini, Roberto (1996). *Oltre il muro, La vera storia di Mucca Pazza*, Roma: Franco Muzzio Editore.

Marchesini, Roberto (1998). *Animali di città.* Como: Red Edizioni.

Marchesini, Roberto (2013), "A Re-examination of Epistemological Paradigms Describing Animal Behavior in 8 Points". *Relations*, 1: 69–77.

Marchesini, Roberto (2017). *Over the Human, Post-humanism and the Concept of Animal Epiphany.* Berlin: Springer.

Marchesini, Roberto (2018a). *Beyond Anthropocentrism, Thoughts for a Post-Human Philosophy.* Udine: Mimesis International.

Marchesini, Roberto (2018b). *Tecnosfera*, Roma: Castelvecchi.

Marchesini, Roberto (2020). *Essere un corpo*, Modena: Stem Mucchi Editore.

Margulis, Lynn (1999). *Symbiotic Planet: A New Look at Evolution*, New York: Basic Books.

Mariotti, Antonella (2019). "2019: un anno di fuoco". *La Stampa*. https://www
.lastampa.it/tuttogreen/2019/12/05/news/wwf-2019-un-anno-di-fuoco-in-
fumo-milioni-di-ettari-di-foresta-1.38072183
Mason, Jim (2005). *An Unnatural Order, The Roots of Our Destruction of
Nature*. New York: Lantern Books.
Mayr, Ernst (1982). *The Growth of Biological Thought*. Cambridge, USA:
Belknap Press of Harvard University Press.
Mazzino, Francesca & Ghersi, Adriana (2003). *Per un atlante dei paesaggi
italiani*. Firenze: Alinea editrice.
McConnachie, James & Tudge, Robin (2005). *The Rough Guide to Conspiracy
Theories*. London: Rough Guide.
McLuhan, Marshall (1964). *Understanding Media: The Extension of Man*.
New York: McGraw Hill.
McQuivey, James (2013). *Digital Disruption: Unleashing the Next Wave of
Innovation*, Seattle: Amazon Publishing.
Menachery, Vineet D. et al. (2015). "A SARS-like Cluster of Circulating Bata
Coronaviruses Shows Potential for Human Emergence". *Nature Medicine*,
21: 1508–1513.
Merleau-Ponty, Maurice (2013). *Phenomenology of Perception*. London:
Routledge.
Midgley, Mary B. (1978). *Beast and Man: The Roots of Human Nature*.
London: Routledge.
Monod, Jacques (1970). *Le hasard et la nécessité*. Paris: Le Seuil.
Moore, Jason W. (2014). "The End of Cheap Nature. Or How I Learned
to Stop Worrying about The Environment and Love the Crisis of
Capitalism". In Suter, Christian and Chase-Dunn, Christopher, (eds.),
*Structures of the World Political Economy and the Future Global
Conflict and Cooperation*. Berlin: LIT Verlag. pp. 285–314.
Moore, Jason W. (ed.) (2016). *Anthropocene or Capitalocene, Nature, History
and the Crisis of Capitalism*. Okland: PM Press.
Morreale, Emiliano (2009). *L'invenzione della Nostalgia*, Roma: Donzelli.
Nicolis, Gregory & Prigogine, Ilya (1977). *Self-Organization in Nonequilibrium
System, from Dissipative Structures to Order Through Fluctuations*.
New York: John Wiley and Sons.
Nikkelen, Sanne W.C. et al. (2014). "Media Use And Adhd-related Behaviors In
Children And Adolescents: A Meta-analysis". *Developmental Psychology*,
5: 2228–2241.
O'Farrell, Clare (2020). "Theoretical Puppets: Foucault on the
Coronavirus, Biopolitics, and the 'Apparatus of Security'". *Foucault
News*. https://michel-foucault.com/2020/04/12/theoretical-puppets-fou

cault-on-the-coronavirus-biopolitics-and-the-apparatus-of-security-2020/

O'Malley, Maureen A. (2016). "The Ecological Virus". *Studies in History and Philosophy of Science Part C: Studies in History and Philosophy of Biological and Biomedical Sciences*, 59: 71–79.

Odling-Smee, John F. (1988). "Niche Constructing Phenotypes". In Plotkin, Henry C. (ed.). *The Role of Behaviour in Evolution.* Cambridge: MIT Press.

Odum, Eugen P. & Barret, Gary W. (2005). *Fundamentals of Ecology.* Belmont, CA: Thomson Brooks-Cole.

Passmore, John (1974). *Man's Responsibility for Nature.* London: Duckworth.

Paul, Gregory & Cox, Earl (1996). *Beyond Humanity: CyberEvolution and Future Minds.* Boston: Charles River Media.

Paul, Ian A. (2020a). *The Corona Reboot*, (www.ianalanpaul.com/the-corona-reboot Accessed November 2, 2020).

Paul, Ian A. (2020b). *Ten Premises for a Pandemic*, (www.ianalanpaul.com/ten-premises-for-a-pandemic Accessed November 2, 2020).

Pennetta, Anna L. (2019). *Bullismo, cyberbullismo e nuove forme di devianza.* Torino: Giappichelli Editore.

Perniola, Mario (1994). *Il sex appeal dell'inorganico.* Torino: Einaudi.

Pfister, Wally (2014). *Transcendence*, United State.

Piaget, Jean (1997). *The Principles of Genetic Epistemology.* London: Routledge.

Pico della Mirandola (1942 [1496]), *Oratio de hominis dignitate.* Firenze: Vallecchi.

Pievani, Telmo (2019). *La Terra dopo di noi.* Milano: ContrastoBooks.

Piva, Gianfranco et al. (1999). *"Recent Progress in Animal Production Science." Future Prospects for the Non-Therapeutics use of Antibiotics.* Milano: Franco Angeli.

Prigogine, Ilya & Stengers, Isabelle (1979). *La Nouvelle alliance, Métamorphose de la science.* Paris: Édition Gallimard.

Quammen, David (2012). *Spillover, Animal Infections and the Next Human Pandemic.* New York: W.W Norton & Company.

Raymond Kurzweil (2005). *The Singularity is Near.* New York: Viking.

Renner, Michael (ed.) (2013). *Vital Sign, The Trends that are Shaping Our Future.* Washington: World Watch Insitute.

Report. Food and Agriculture Organization of the United Nations (February 2019). *Current Worldwide Annual Meat Consumption.*

Ricci, Carla (2008). *Hikikomori: adolescenti in volontaria reclusione.* Milano: Franco Angeli.

Rifkin, Jeremy (1993). *Beyond Beef: The Rise and Fall of the Cattle Culture*. London: Plume.

Rivoltella, Pier Cesare & Rossi, Pier Giuseppe (2019), *Il corpo e la macchina, Tecnologia, cultura, educazione*. Brescia: Scholé.

Sachs, Jeffrey (2011). *Common Wealth, Economics for a Crowded Planet*, London: Penguin.

Sanchez, Travis (2019). "Wet Markets and Food Safety: TripAdvisor for Improved Global Digital Surveillance". *JMIR Public Health and Surveillance*, 5: e11477.

Schaeffer, Jean-Marie (2007). *La fin de l'exception humaine*. Paris: Gallimard.

Scheper-Hughes, Nancy (2000). "The Global Traffic in Human Organs". *Current Anthropology*, 41: 191–224.

Schopenhauer, Arthur (1851). *Parerga and Paralipomena*. Berlin: Druck und Verlag von A. W. Hayn.

Schrödinger, Erwin (1940). *What is Life?*. Cambridge: Cambridge University Press.

Shantser, V. (1973). *The Anthropogenic System*. Great Soviet Encyclopedia.

Simondon, Gilbert (1958). *Du mode d'existence des objets techniques*. Paris: Éditions Aubier.

Sirucek, Stefan (2014). "Ancient 'Giant Virus' Revived from Siberian Permafrost". *National Geographic*, 3. https://www.nationalgeographic.com/news/2014/3/140303-giant-virus-permafrost-siberia-pithovirus-pandoravirus-science

Skinner, Burrhus (1938). *The Behavior of Organisms*. New York: Appleton-Century Company.

Sloterdijk, Peter (2014). *You Must Change Your Life*. Cambridge: Polity.

Smith, Adam (1776). *An Inquiry into the Nature and Causes of the Wealth of Nations*.

Smith, Robert L. & Smith Thomas M. (2006). *Elements of Ecology*. Harlow: Pearson Education.

Smith, Wesley J. (2002). *Culture of Death: the Assault on Medical Ethics in America*, San Francisco: Encounter Books.

Snowden, Frank M. (2019). *Epidemics and Society: From the Black Death to the Present*. United States: Yale University Press.

Solidoro, Adriano (2020). "Guerra alle metafore di guerra al coronavirus". *Il Manifesto*, 4. https://ilmanifesto.it/guerra-alle-metafore-di-guerra-sul-coronavirus

Solove, Daniel J. (2004). *The Digital Person: Technology and Privacy in the Information Age*. New York: New York University Press.

Sontag, Susan (1978). *Illness as Metaphor.* New York: Farrar, Straus and Giroux.

Spilsbury, Richard (2011). *Deforestation,* New York: The Rosen Publishing Group.

The Guardian (2009). *Meat consumption per capita.* https://www.theguardian.com/environment/datablog/2009/sep/02/meat-consumption-per-capita-climate-change

Thoreau, Henry David (1957). *Walden.* Boston: Houghton Mifflin. First edition 1854.

Tibon-Cornillot, Michel & Andremont, Antoine (2007). *Le Triomphe des Bactéries: La Fin des Antibiotiques?.* Paris: Max Milo Éditions.

Tilocca, Bruno, et al. (2020). "Molecular Basis Of Covid-19 Relationship In Different Species: A One Health Perspective". *Microbes and Infection,* 22: 218–220.

Van Hoof, Elke (9 April 2020). "Lockdown Is the World's Biggest Psychological Experiment – and We Will Pay the Price". *The World Economic Forum.* https://www.weforum.org/agenda/2020/04/this-is-the-psychological-side-of-the-covid-19-pandemic-that-were-ignoring

von Bertalanffy, Ludwig (1976). *General System Theory: Foundations, Development, Applications.* New York: George Braziller.

von Uexküll, Jakob J. (2010). *A Foray Into the Worlds of Animals and Humans: With A Theory of Meaning.* Minneapolis: University of Minnesota Press.

Weisman, Alan (2008). *The World Without Us.* London: Virgin Books.

Wilen, Tracey (2018). *Digital Disruption: the Future of Work, Skills, Leadership,* New York: Peter Lang Pub. Inc.

Wilson, Edward O. (2017). *The Origins of Creativity.* United States: WW Norton & C.

World Health Organization, "Mental health and Covid-19". https://www.who.int/teams/mental-health-and-substance-use/covid-1

Žižek, Slavoj (2020). *Virus.* Milano: Ponte alle Grazie.

Acknowledgments

I would like to express my special gratitude to Serenella Iovino, Timo Maran, and Louise Westling for their help and encouragement in writing this book and to the translator Sarah De Sanctis, who knows my work very well.

Cambridge Elements ≡

Environmental Humanities

Louise Westling
University of Oregon

Louise Westling is an American scholar of literature and environmental humanities who was a founding member of the Association for the Study of Literature and Environment and its President in 1998. She has been active in the international movement for environmental cultural studies, teaching and writing on landscape imagery in literature, critical animal studies, biosemiotics, phenomenology, and deep history.

Serenella Iovino
University of North Carolina at Chapel Hill

Serenella Iovino is Professor of Italian Studies and Environmental Humanities at the University of North Carolina at Chapel Hill. She has written on a wide range of topics, including environmental ethics and ecocritical theory, bioregionalism and landscape studies, ecofeminism and posthumanism, comparative literature, eco-art, and the Anthropocene.

Timo Maran
University of Tartu

Timo Maran is an Estonian semiotician and poet. Maran is Professor of Ecosemiotics and Environmental Humanities and Head of the Department of Semiotics at the University of Tartu. His research interests are semiotic relations of nature and culture, Estonian nature writing, zoosemiotics and species conservation, semiotics of biological mimicry.

About the Series

The environmental humanities is a new transdisciplinary complex of approaches to the embeddedness of human life and culture in all the dynamics that characterize the life of the planet. These approaches reexamine our species' history in light of the intensifying awareness of drastic climate change and ongoing mass extinction. To engage this reality, Cambridge Elements in Environmental Humanities builds on the idea of a more hybrid and participatory mode of research and debate, connecting critical and creative fields.

Cambridge Elements ☰

Environmental Humanities

Printed in the United States
By Bookmasters